With be

Joan

Oct. 2022

COURAGE AND CONVICTION

COURAGE AND CONVICTION

Pius XII, the Bridgettine nuns,
and the rescue of Jews
Mother Riccarda Hambrough and
Mother Katherine Flanagan

JOANNA BOGLE

GRACEWING

First published in 2013 by
Gracewing
2 Southern Avenue
Leominster
Herefordshire HR6 0QF
United Kingdom
www.gracewing.co.uk

No part of this publication may be reproduced, stored in a
retrieval system, or transmitted in any form or by any means,
electronic, mechanical, photocopying, recording or otherwise,
without the written permission of the publisher.

The rights of Joanna Bogle to be identified as the author of this
work have been asserted in accordance with the Copyright,
Designs and Patents Act 1988.

© 2013 Joanna Bogle

ISBN 978 085244 744 4

Typeset by Gracewing

Cover design by Bernardita Peña Hurtado

CONTENTS

ACKNOWLEDGEMENTS

 AM INDEBTED TO a number of people, with regard to assistance in finding out about the Hambrough family: Lord Coleridge, Fay Brown and the Ventnor History Society, Vanessa Coutts, Sue Comrie-Thompson, and Fiona Mercey. Lord Coleridge married Basil Hambrough's daughter. Sue Comrie-Thomson is the great-granddaughter of John Comrie-Thomson who was the defence lawyer in the Ardlamount case, and sent me much useful material. Fay Brown and Vanessa Coutts provided a great deal of information about the Hambroughs and Steephill Castle, and Fiona Mercey about Basil Hambrough. I am very grateful to them all. I also express warmest thanks to Father Ray Blake of St Mary Magdalen's church, Brighton, to Father John Henry of St Gregory's, Earlsfield, and to Fr Michael Clifton, retired archivist of the Catholic diocese of Southwark. I am particularly indebted to Mr Piero Piperno who spent an afternoon with me at the Bridgettine convent in Rome, talking about his wartime memories, and to Father Nicoletti MJ who translated for us. I am hugely grateful to Mother Thekla, of the Bridgettine community, who has given me much assistance. Thanks, too, to the Bridgettines at Maryvale Institute, Birmingham, whose support and encouragement has meant a a great deal.

15 August 2013, Solemnity of the Assumption

CHAPTER ONE

N THE DARKEST period of German and European history, an insane racist ideology, born of neo-paganism, gave rise to the attempt, planned and systematically carried out by the regime, to exterminate European Jewry... millions of Jews—men, women and children—were put to death in the gas chambers and ovens.[1]

At the time of the horror of the Holocaust, when six million Jewish people perished in the Nazi extermination programme, there were people who tried to offer Jews shelter and protection, risking—and sometimes giving—their own lives in doing so. At Yad Vashem, the Holocaust memorial in Israel, some of these people are honoured. One of them is Mother Elisabeth Hesselblad, a Swedish woman who had established the Bridgettine order of nuns in Rome in the early years of the 20th century and who, during World War II, hid Jewish families in the convent, successfully protecting them and saving their lives. She has now formally been declared Blessed by the Catholic Church—in a ceremony carried out by Pope John Paul in April 2000.

Of course Mother Elisabeth did not work alone. She was the head of a community of nuns, and her deputy, Mother Riccarda Hambrough, was a key figure in helping to save the Jews, arranging food in the difficult wartime conditions, sorting out the difficulties that arose day by day, keeping everything secret, restoring morale when tensions arose.

Mother Riccarda was English. She was born Catherine Hambrough, a member of a well-connected family which had once owned Steephill Castle on the Isle of Wight. Together with another Bridgettine nun, Katherine Flanagan, she may one day be formally declared a saint. The process for their Beatification has been introduced in the Catholic Church. Both served the Church and the wider human community in different ways. But before we explore their stories, it is necessary to look at the bigger picture of Jewish people in wartime Rome, and those who tried to help them.

In the middle of the 20th century anyone viewing the relationship between Christians and Jews in Rome down the years would have to state that it had been a troubled one. For many years—long vanished by the mid-20th century—Jews had been made to live in a restricted area by the river. They were banned from most jobs and professions, and at one stage were made to attend sermons every week, in a church bearing Scriptural verses exhorting them to conversion. In 1846 Pius IX ordered the removal of the walls and gates of the ghetto, but laws restricting various aspects of Jewish life were still enforced in the Papal States.

In the late 19th century, with Italian unification, the last vestiges of the ghetto were abolished. Over the next years social changes were rapid and strong social, business, and neighbourhood contacts between Christians and Jews flourished.

Everyday life in Rome in the 1920s and 30s, centred on the realities of work and home and school, for Christians and Jews alike. Many might have assumed that modern life was opening up new opportunities for everyone, with many old barriers being dissolved. But this was not the case: in Germany the Nazi came to power in the 1930s and in Italy the Fascists. The Jews in Rome, facing the most tragic chapter of their long history, would find that the Church was their ally and a source of hope.

Cardinal Eugenio Pacelli was elected as Pope in March 1939. He knew Germany well, having been Nuncio there for some years, and he saw the danger as the Nazi party rose to power. In 1938, as a Cardinal he had drafted the letter *Mit Brennender Sorge* ('With burning anxiety') which was signed by the then Pope, Pius XI and read out in all the Catholic churches in Germany, denouncing the Nazi ideology.

Following the outbreak of war, Hitler was extremely concerned about this anti-Nazi Pope whose views were so close to those of the western Allies. Joachim von Ribbentrop was sent to talk to him. Dr. Joseph Lichten, a Polish Jew who worked first as a diplomat and then for the Jewish Anti-Defamation League of B'nai B'rith, would later describe how the meeting went:

> Von Ribbentrop, granted a formal audience on March 11, 1940, went into a lengthy harangue on the invincibility of the Third Reich, the inevitability of a Nazi victory, and the futility of papal alignment with the enemies of the Führer. Pius XII heard von Ribbentrop out politely and impassively. Then he opened an enormous ledger on his desk and, in his perfect German, began to recite a catalogue of the persecutions inflicted by the Third Reich in Poland, listing the date, place, and precise details of each crime. The audience was terminated; the Pope's position was clearly unshakable.[2]

The majority of Italian Jews—some 80 per cent - survived the Second World War, in the years when, across the rest of Europe, 80 per cent of Jews died. Rabbi Pinchas Lapide notes that Pius XII and the Catholic Church rescued the largest number of Jews of any relief group in Europe—some 700,000, far more than the Red Cross or any of the Jewish agencies.[3]

Italy was initially regarded as a safe place for Jews who attempted to get there from other parts of Europe. In particular, there was hope and help from the Church and specifically from the Vatican. In 2010 Robert Adler recalled how his father, Hugo Adler, was taken into the Vatican in 1941 and was hidden for five weeks. During that time, he met personally with Pope Pius XII on several occasions. A Vatican network then enabled Hugo to travel through France, into Spain, from where he was able to leave for the Dominican Republic. Robert concluded that his father would have died if Pius XII had not intervened.[4]

The political situation in Italy during the war was complex. The Fascist Party was not so fully rooted in the same anti-Jewish fanaticism that hallmarked the Nazis—in fact there were some Jews in the party in its early days. Later Benito Mussolini the Fascist leader imposed the Manifesto of Race, modelled on the Nazi Nuremberg Laws—this stripped Jews of their Italian citizenship. But the main danger to Jews came after Mussolini's government surrendered to the Allies and Hitler's forces effectively took Italy, 'rescuing' Mussolini from his mountain haven and establishing him at the head of a puppet government.

Italy had not deported any Jews 'to the east' (namely to Poland and Ukraine, where the death-camps were), and indeed those who lived in areas of Europe that

Italy controlled, such as Croatia, had been safe. But after 1943 things changed and Jews were at risk of their lives. Many fled to Rome from other parts of Italy, knowing that the Church might be able to protect them. This indeed proved to be the case.

> The Pope sent out the order that religious buildings were to give refuge to Jews, even at the price of great personal sacrifice on the part of their occupants; he released monasteries and convents from the cloister rule forbidding entry into these religious houses to all but a few specified outsiders, so that they could be used as hiding places. Thousands of Jews—the figures run from 4,000 to 7,000—were hidden, fed, clothed, and bedded in the 180 known places of refuge in Vatican City, churches and basilicas, Church administrative buildings, and parish houses. Unknown numbers of Jews were sheltered in Castel Gandolfo, the site of the Pope's summer residence, private homes, hospitals, and nursing institutions; and the Pope took personal responsibility for the care of the children of Jews deported from Italy.[5]

The scale of rescue work was huge. Rabbi G. Dalin writes:

> In the months Rome was under German occupation, Pius XII instructed Italy's clergy to save lives by all means... Beginning in October 1943, Pius asked churches and convents throughout Italy to shelter Jews. As a result—and despite the fact that Mussolini and the Fascists yielded to Hitler's demand for deportations—many Italian Catholics defied the German orders.

In Rome, 155 convents and monasteries sheltered some five thousand Jews. At least three
thousand found refuge at the pope's summer
residence at Castel Gandolfo. Sixty Jews lived
for nine months at the Gregorian University,
and many were sheltered in the cellar of the
pontifical biblical institute. Hundreds found
sanctuary within the Vatican itself. Following
Pius's instructions, individual Italian priests,
monks, nuns, cardinals, and bishops were
instrumental in preserving thousands of Jewish
lives. Cardinal Boetto of Genoa saved at least
eight hundred. The bishop of Assisi hid three
hundred Jews for over two years. The bishop
of Campagna and two of his relatives saved 961
more in Fiume.[6]

The former Chief Rabbi of Rome would later recall
'The Holy Father sent by hand a letter to the bishops
instructing them to lift the enclosure from convents
and monasteries, so that they could become refuges
for the Jews. I know of one convent where the sisters
slept in the basement, giving up their beds so Jewish
refugees. In face of this charity, the fate of so many of
the persecuted is especially tragic.'[7]

The main round-up of Jews in Rome by the Nazis
began on the evening of 15 October 1943. No warning
had been given, and many of those arrested had been
confident that they were safe in Rome. The former
Chief Rabbi later wrote:

The number of Jews was small, and the
Germans had little to gain from their elimina-
tion. It was known that the German army was
opposed to their persecution on political
grounds. But reason had little hold on the SS,
and the question was whether or not they could

> be restrained. My whole experience argued against the possibility of their being restrained more than temporarily.[8]

Shortly before the German army reached Rome he contacted the leaders of the Jewish community and urged that people be helped to disperse and go into hiding—already it was known that there were many families that would help and that shelter could also be found through the Church. But he was not believed— assurances had been given and it was felt that everyone should remain calm and that the Rabbi should try to show confidence and hope. Relationships with the Italian authorities were good, and there were many strong personal friendships between Christians and Jews in Rome. The two presidents of the Jewish community simply did not share the Rabbi's fears. 'Reason and logic were on their side. Had not the "powerful" Italian-constituted Authorities given explicit assurances? Is it not true that in Rome not a single Hebrew had been hurt?'[9]

But the round-up of 15–16 October opened a new and grim chapter. One thousand people were arrested and taken to a military college to await deportation - most would perish in Auschwitz.

The Pope, like others, had been given detailed reassurances—indeed it was widely known that the sense of safety felt by Jews in Rome was due to the fact that any deportations from the city would bring an immediate denouncement from him. On the morning of 16 October he heard about the arrests - Princess Enza Pignatelli Aragona Cortes, who had been alerted by a Jewish friend, rushed to the Vatican. The Pope immediately sent a protest to the German ambassador to the Vatican, Ernst von Weizsacker.

The protest was delivered by the Pope's secretary of State Cardinal Maglione who told Weiszacker 'It is sad for the Holy Father, sad beyond imagination, that here in Rome, under the very eyes of the Common Father, so many people should suffer only because they belong to a specific race.'

This did have an effect and the deportations were stopped — Rome's remaining Jews now had a chance of survival. The Pope was already giving instructions, as mentioned, to all the convents, churches and religious institutions to open up for Jewish refugees. According to the available records, 'of the 5,715 Roman Jews listed by the Germans for deportation, 4,715 were given shelter in more than 150 Catholic institutions in the city; of these, 477 were given sanctuary within the confines of the Vatican itself.'[10]

The British ambassador to the Vatican later reported back to Britain: 'Vatican intervention thus seems to have been effective in saving numbers of these unfortunate people.' But it had been too late for the first thousand arrested — only ten of those taken on 15 October would survive the concentration camps.

Martin Gilbert notes:

> As the Germans began deporting Jews from other parts of northern Italy, the Pope opened his summer estate at Castel Gandolfo to take in several thousand (women had their babies in the Pope's apartment) and authorized monasteries throughout the German-occupied areas of Italy to do likewise. As a result, while the Germans managed to seize and deport a further 7,000 Italian Jews to their deaths, 35,000 survived the war — one of the highest ratios of those rescued of any country.[11]

Pius' assistant in carrying out the practical—and dangerous—work of contacting convents and other institutions, raising funds, and making all the various necessary arrangements was Cardinal Giovanni Battista Montini. He would later go on to be Archbishop of Milan and, eventually be elected to the Papacy as Paul VI. Martin Gilbert comments:

> When the government of Israel asked him, in 1955, to accept an award for his rescue work during the Holocaust, Montini replied: 'All I did was my duty. And besides I only acted upon orders from the Holy Father.'[12]

In 1944, the Chief Rabbi of Jerusalem, Isaac Herzog, sent the Pope a message of thanks: 'The people of Israel will never forget what His Holiness and his illustrious delegates, inspired by the eternal principles of religion which form the very foundations of true civilization, are doing for us unfortunate brothers and sisters in the most tragic hour of our history, which is living proof of divine Providence in this world.'[13]

When peace came, there was great Jewish gratitude for the work of Pius XII and the Church in saving Jewish lives. In October 1945 the World Jewish Congress donated $20,000 to Vatican charities. According to the *New York Times* (12 October 1945), the gift was 'made in recognition of the work of the Holy See in rescuing Jews from Fascist and Nazi persecution.'[14]

When Pius XII died in 1958, tributes were paid to him around the world. Mrs Golda Meir, later to become Prime Minister of Israel, was then the country's Foreign Minister and said: 'When fearful martyrdom came to our people in the decade of Nazi terror, the voice of the Pope was raised for the victims. The life of our times was enriched by a voice speaking out on the great moral truths above the tumult of daily conflict.'[15]

The Jewish Chronicle (10 October 1958) pointed out in a leader:

> Adherents of all faiths will recall how Pius XII faced the responsibilities of his exalted office with courage and devotion... Confronted by the monstrous cruelties of Nazism, Fascism and Communism, he repeatedly proclaimed the virtues of humanity and compassion... This attitude found practical expression during the Nazi occupation of Rome ... when many hundreds of fugitive Jews found sanctuary in the Vatican from massacre by the Nazis. Such actions will always be remembered.[16]

In 1965, the Church, at the Second Vatican Council, under the leadership of Pope Paul VI, issued the official declaration *Nostra Aetate*, stating

> in her rejection of every persecution against any man, the Church, mindful of the patrimony she shares with the Jews and moved not by political reasons but by the Gospel's spiritual love, decries hatred, persecutions, displays of anti-Semitism, directed against Jews at any time and by anyone.[17]

The Declaration also explicitly repudiated the notion that the Jewish people were responsible for the death of Christ—an idea that had, up to that time, been taught by some Catholic clergy, teachers, and publications. To this end *Nostra Aetate* states:

> what happened in His [Christ's] passion cannot be charged against all the Jews, without distinction, then alive, nor against the Jews of today.

> Although the Church is the new people of God,
> the Jews should not be presented as rejected or
> accursed by God, as if this followed from the
> Holy Scriptures. All should see to it, then, that
> in catechetical work or in the preaching of the
> word of God they do not teach anything that
> does not conform to the truth of the Gospel and
> the spirit of Christ.[18]

Pope John Paul II and Pope Benedict XVI both paid
particular attention to the Church's bond with the
Jewish people, emphasising that this is something of
crucial importance and that it must flourish. Pope John
Paul became the first Pope since St Peter to visit a
synagogue.

> Throughout 1,900 years of a tortured relation-
> ship, no Pope had ever set foot in the Syna-
> gogue of Rome, although John XXXIII had once
> had his car stopped so that he could bless the
> Roman Jews leaving their Sabbath worship. On
> April 13, 1986, John Paul II drove from the
> Vatican, across the Tiber, and down the Lun-
> gotevere, to change history. The Bishop of Rome
> was going to the Synagogue of Rome to meet
> the Roman Jewish community at their place of
> worship.[19]

Pope—now Blessed—John Paul II brought to his
Papacy a deep understanding of the crucial need to
forge a new relationship with the Jewish people: he
had experienced the Nazi occupation of Poland, and
one of his closest boyhood friends was Jewish, Jerzy
Kluger. The concentration camp of Auschwitz lies not
far from the city of Krakow, and as Archbishop he had
visited it and prayed there in mourning.

Now in the Rome Synagogue he sought to open a new chapter. Catholics must learn that Judaism was not 'extrinsic' to the Christian faith but 'intrinsic': 'With Judaism, therefore, we have a relationship which we do not have with any other religion. You are our dearly beloved brothers and, in a certain way, it could be said that you are our elder brothers.'

He spoke frankly about the realities of the past, and the relationship between the Church and the Jews:

> Certainly, we cannot and should not forget that the historical circumstances of the past were very different from those that have laboriously matured over the centuries. The general acceptance of a legitimate plurality on the social, civil and religious levels has been arrived at with great difficulty. Nevertheless, a consideration of centuries-long cultural conditioning could not prevent us from recognizing that the acts of discrimination, unjustified limitation of religion freedom, oppression also on the level of civil freedom in regard to the Jews were, from an objective point of view, gravely deplorable manifestations. Yes, once again, through myself, the Church, in the words of the well-known Declaration *Nostra Aetate*, 'deplores the hatred, persecutions and displays of anti-Semitism directed against the Jews at any time and by anyone' I repeat: 'by anyone'.[20]

The Pope then spoke about the Holocaust, and about his visit as pope to Auschwitz. In that grim place, Jews from across Europe met their deaths.

> The Jewish community of Rome too paid a high price in blood. And it was surely a significant gesture that in those dark years of racial perse-cution the doors of our religious houses, of our

churches, of the Roman Seminary, of buildings belonging to the Holy See and of Vatican City itself were thrown open to offer refuge and safety to so many Jews of Rome being hunted by their persecutors.[21]

When Benedict XVI succeeded Pope John Paul in 2005 he made a synagogue visit a priority on his first visit to his native Germany after his election. Later he visited Yad Vashem in Jersalem and, like his predecessor, he accepted an invitation to the Rome Synagogue. Here, he laid flowers at a plaque commemorating the Jews who were rounded up and taken to concentration camps and death, and spoke of the Holocaust:

> Here in this place, how could we not remember the Roman Jews who were snatched from their homes, before these very walls, and who with tremendous brutality were killed at Auschwitz? How could one ever forget their faces, their names, their tears, the desperation faced by these men, women and children? The extermination of the people of the Covenant of Moses, at first announced, then systematically programmed and put into practice in Europe under the Nazi regime, on that day tragically reached as far as Rome. Unfortunately, many remained indifferent, but many, including Italian Catholics, sustained by their faith and by Christian teaching, reacted with courage, often at risk of their lives, opening their arms to assist the Jewish fugitives who were being hunted down, and earning perennial gratitude. The Apostolic See itself provided assistance, often in a hidden and discreet way.[22]

At Yad Vashem he had emphasised that each of those
who were killed had a name, and each was infinitely
precious:

> I have come to stand in silence before this
> monument, erected to honour the memory of
> the millions of Jews killed in the horrific tragedy
> of the *Shoah*. They lost their lives, but they will
> never lose their names: these are indelibly
> etched in the hearts of their loved ones, their
> surviving fellow prisoners, and all those deter-
> mined never to allow such an atrocity to dis-
> grace mankind again. Most of all, their names
> are forever fixed in the memory of Almighty
> God... May the names of these victims never
> perish! May their suffering never be denied,
> belittled or forgotten! And may all people of
> goodwill remain vigilant in rooting out from
> the heart of man anything that could lead to
> tragedies such as this![23]

Telling the story of Christians who helped to save and
shelter Jews during the Nazi era is a way of keeping
memories alive, and is also important for the future,
honouring the important bond between Christian and
Jews.

It is not easy to collect together the details of the
stories: hiding people in wartime is by definition
something that must be done with secrecy and discretion. Many of those who were hidden—or who were
helping to hide people—did not know about other
occupants of the house, or did not know their real
names or circumstances. After the War, people wanted
to rebuild their lives, to survive the new hardships of
the postwar era in a battered Europe, and to discover
new hope. Many did not want to tell their stories until
long years later.

The story of the Bridgettine nuns in Rome is just a small part of the jigsaw of all of this. The sisters did not think of themselves as heroic, and indeed not all the Sisters in the convent in the Piazza Farnese knew that the guests they were sheltering in 1944–45 were Jewish and that everyone in the building was at risk of being arrested and killed. Only now, with the perspective of history, can we see that those years were part of an unfolding saga that would include a whole new perspective on Catholic-Jewish relations, opening up new dimensions with the Second Vatican Council and the initiatives of Popes John Paul II and Benedict.

> As Christians and Jews, following the example of the faith of Abraham, we are called to be a blessing to the world. This is the common task awaiting us. It is therefore necessary for us, Christians and Jews, to first be a blessing to one another.[24]

Notes

[1] Pope Benedict XVI, *Address to Cologne Synagogue* (19 August 2005).

[2] J. Lichten, 'A Question of Moral Judgement: Pius XII and the Jews' in R. Graham SJ (ed.), *Pius XII and the Holocaust* (New Rochelle, New York: Catholic League for Religious and Civil Rights, 1988), p. 107.

[3] P. E. Lapide, *Three Popes and the Jews* (New York: Hawthorn, 1967), p. 215.

[4] Zenit news agency (2 November 2010)

[5] Lichten, 'A Question of Moral Judgement: Pius XII and the Jews', p. 107.

[6] D. G. Dalin, *The Weekly Standard* (26 February 2001), Vol 6 Number 23.

[7] E. Zolli, *Why I became a Catholic* (New York: Roman Catholic

Books, 1953), p. 141.

8   *Ibid.* p. 140.

9   *Ibid.* p. 152.

10 M. Gilbert, 'Hitler's Pope?' *The American Spectator* (July/August 2006). On the Internet at: spectator.org/archives/2006/08/18/hitlers-pope.

11 *Ibid.*

12 *Ibid.*

13 Message sent by Rabbi Isaac Herzog 28 February, 1944.

14 D. Cavalli, *Inside the Vatican* (October 2000), p. 72–77.

15 *Ibid.*

16 Quoted in J. Frain, *The Cross and the Third Reich* (Oxford: Family Publications, 2009), p. 313.

17 Vatican II, *Nostra Aetate* , Declaration on the Relation of the Church to non-Christian religions (28 October 1965), 4.

18 *Ibid.*

19 G. Weigel, *Witness to Hope* (London: HarperCollins, 1999) p. 484.

20 Pope John Paul II, *Address at the Synagogue of Rome* (13 April 1986). See also *Nostra Aetate*, 4.

21 *Ibid.*

22 Pope Benedict XVI, *Address at the Synagogue of Rome* (17 January 2010).

23 Pope Benedict XVI, *Address at Yad Vashem Memorial* (11 May 2009).

24 Pope John Paul II, *Message on the 50th anniversary of the Warsaw Ghetto Uprising* (6 April 1993).

CHAPTER TWO

N THE 19TH century, the Isle of Wight became very fashionable. Steephill Castle was built by the Hambrough family at Ventnor in 1833. All that is now left of it are some walls, incorporated into a development of hilltop houses, and a gateway that once led to the stable block, with posts that still show remnants of a family crest. The castle itself was pulled down in the 1960s.

The man who built Steephill Castle was John Hambrough, a noted botanist. The Hambroughs were a wealthy family, with banking interests in London and New York. Steephill Castle stood on a commanding site overlooking the sea. It was a good time to be acquiring property on the island. Queen Victoria and Prince Albert built Osborne House as a holiday home near Cowes, and over the next years a number of noted people were to live on the Isle of Wight or make regular visits: Alfred Lord Tennyson, Charles Dickens, Sir Edward Elgar. The railway and the ferry service from the mainland were to prove crucial in popularising the island, although John Hambrough led opposition to the extension of the railway to Ventnor and seems to have been successful in delaying its arrival by about ten years.

The Hambroughs had come from Hanwell in Middlesex. John Hambrough never actually saw Steephill Castle—by the time it was fully completed in 1835, he had become blind. So he never viewed it in its final form, with his initials intertwined with those of his wife Sophia on the arched entrance over the drive, and his own initials and arms over the main doorway with the word "Foresight". But he made Steephill Castle his home for some thirty years, established his family there, and built a church and a school for the local people. The church still thrives today. It was named after St Catherine because this was his mother's name. There is a memorial to her in the church:

> In a Vault beneath repose the remains of Catherine Hambrough, who died in this Island, March 18th, 1841. She was relict of John Hambrough Esq, who died May 9th 1831 and was interred in the Family Vault in Hanwell Church Yard, Middlesex... To the revered memory of his departed Parents, an affectionate Son erects this Tablet.[1]

The name Catherine clearly had resonance in the family. John Hambrough's grandson, Windsor John Beauchamp Hambrough married Louise Frances Fisher in 1877 and when a baby daughter was born to them on 10 September 1887 they named her Catherine. She was born in Kensington, and baptised at Christ Church, in the London parish of St Pancras, in November. Catherine Marie Clarice Beauchamp Hambrough was to grow up to have an extraordinary life, and despite being given a string of names at birth was to change her name twice more, even though she never married.

An older brother, Dudley Windsor Hambrough, had been born in 1886 and another, Basil Tudor Vincent Hambrough, was to be born in 1893. But 1887, the year of Catherine's birth, was to prove a difficult one for the family: in December bankruptcy proceedings were begun against her father in the Lincolns Inn Bankruptcy Buildings. In September Steephill Castle had been sold to a Mr Henry Sewell, who owned property in the West Indies. It must have been a sad and humiliating experience for the family. The hospitality at Steephill had been famous: 'Mama and I went to a ball at Mrs Hambrough's Steep Hill Castle' wrote Alice Thompson (later Meynell) in 1865 'I wore a ravishing yellow tarlatan of the palest possible tint...' and on another occasion Alice Thompson's mother wrote 'The H's ball was splendid, a profusion of pink wax lights, a flow of champagne...'[2] They stayed at the Castle and everything was extremely luxurious and comfortable 'Lovely bedroom and fire blazing and Mrs H. so kind.' It was not to last: by the 1870s the Hambroughs had had to leave and put the castle up for rent: in 1874 the Empress of Austria came to stay, with a large party, the castle having been substantially remodelled and redecorated to meet her needs.

The Hambrough family fortunes seem to have been mixed: although they lost their money, they still retained their aristocratic connections and in some cases the lifestyle. Little Catherine Hambrough and her parents certainly did not enjoy the latter: by 1891 they were living at Hove in Sussex. It was here that her parents made a decision that was to have a profound impact on the rest of her life—they joined the Roman Catholic Church. This was a major decision, and one which an increasing number of English people were making: new Catholic churches had been springing up all over the country throughout Queen Victoria's reign, Catholic schools were being established run by newly-founded religious orders, and the Church was experiencing what Cardinal John Henry Newman was to describe as a 'Second Spring' after the devastation and years of persecution that had followed the events of the reigns of Henry VIII and Elizabeth I.

For small Catherine Hambrough, becoming Roman Catholic meant being baptised *sub conditione*—in case the clergyman at the original Anglican baptism had not used the proper formula,[3] it was routine for the baptism to be done again, the priest beginning the ceremony with the words 'If you are not already baptised, I baptise you…' These were not ecumenical days. Whereas four-year old Catherine was simply given conditional baptism, her parents were listed in the parish register as having been brought back from heresy!

All this took place at St Mary Magdalene's church in Brighton on 6 May 1891. The officiating priest was Father George Tatum, himself a convert from the Church of England, who had been received into the Catholic Church by John Henry Newman. And little Catherine was now given a new name—one by which she would be known throughout her childhood and young womanhood, and would carry until she made another major change in her twenties. She became Madeleine, the name clearly having been chosen to link with the Brighton church.

When Madeleine was small, the family name was spread all over the newspapers in a murder case that caught the public imagination. It involved a cousin, Windsor Dudley Cecil Hambrough, who in 1894 was shot in mysterious circumstances while out with his tutor Alfred Monson and a friend, Edward Sweeney.

The three had gone out shooting rabbits while staying at the Ardlamont Estate in Argyllshire. A butler from the house came across the corpse of Hambrough, who had been killed by a three-inch horizontal wound behind his left ear. His two companions were nearby, cleaning their guns. There was immediate suspicion of murder, because just a few days earlier Monson had persuaded Hambrough to take out life insurance policies in the name of Mrs Monson for a large sum. In the ensuing court case, Ardlamount servants, representatives from the insurance company, a gun maker, and the police, all gave evidence. It emerged that Hambrough had had a narrow escape from death only days earlier when a boat in which he was fishing sank—he was known to be a non-swimmer and he almost drowned. Evidence seemed to point to Monson having drilled a hole in the boat before encouraging Hambrough to board.

The case attracted enormous interest, not least because the other character involved, Edward Sweeney, alias Scott, had disappeared and there was a £200 reward for his capture. Eventually, Monson was cleared of the murder thanks to an effective defence lawyer. But three years later he was imprisoned for an insurance fraud, and in 1896 his wife Agnes sued him for failing to support her and their six children. He responded by suing her for divorce, citing Hambrough as the co-respondent.

The extensive Hambrough family must all have been embarrassed by this publicity over a tragedy. Although no longer living in grand style on the Isle of Wight, they were still well-connected and the young murder victim had been set to attend the Royal Military Academy at Sandhurst until he fell under the influence of Monson who encouraged him not to go.

The whole story had a flavour of faded grandeur and lost hopes.

Meanwhile, young Madeleine Hambrough was emerging from babyhood and was ready for school. Her family moved several times during her childhood. After living at Hove for a time, they moved to Bognor Regis further along the coast, later to Richmond in Surrey and then back to Bognor again.

Perhaps it was this lack of a stable home that encouraged them to send their daughter to a boarding-school—she became a pupil at a convent school established by Sacred Heart nuns at Stanwix in Carlisle. A school so far away seems an odd choice—it may have been that the Sacred Heart nuns were aware of the family's comparative poverty and wanted to help a family of new converts, and offered generous terms. The school was opened in 1892 and Madeleine would have been among the very first pupils. A guidebook to Cumberland in 1901[4] notes that the building had cost some £25,000 and stood in some eleven acres 'tastefully laid out in gardens etc.' It said 'The community consists at the present time of 22 sisters, whose object it is to look after the spiritual and temporal well-being of the young ladies placed under their charge for their education.' Two years later the nuns left for Newcastle and the school closed. The buildings became a reformatory school for boys run by the Presentation Brothers, known as the Chadwick Memorial Industrial School, and then an orphanage, Nazareth House. In 1951 it was sold to the Augustinians who opened a boarding school for boys. Today, the Austin Friars School still flourishes as an independent school no longer under the control of a religious order. St Monica's was added as a junior school in the 1980s and the two schools merged recently to form a co-educational day-school.

When Madeleine completed her education she could not expect to live as a wealthy young lady. Her family background was well-connected but there was no money now. Her brother Basil was set to become an Army officer, and in November 1910 he was formally gazetted as a Second Lieutenant in the 3rd battalion, the Norfolk Regiment.[5] His choice in life had been made—what was hers to be?

In September 1911 Madeleine's father died. She was by then 23 years old, and was not alone in the world as she had her mother and two brothers. The family lived at Sefton Cottage, Bognor Regis. But her father had left just £103 and there was no question of her simply remaining quietly at home. And in any case the world was changing: more jobs and careers were opening up for women and a new century had begun. Madeleine, an enthusiastic young Catholic, would think long and hard about her future. In the end the decision she made was an unusual one: she found inspiration in the life and message of a Swedish noblewoman of the 13th century, and it is to the story of this woman that we must now turn.

Notes

1   Catherine Hambrough had lived her final years at another substantial family property on the island, Westbrook House, near Ryde, standing in some 26 acres of parkland. (It still stands today and is now used as an activity centre for young people run by the Crusaders, a Christian evangelical group).

2   V. Meynell 'Alice Meynell, a Memoir' in H. Noyes *The Isle of Wight Bedside Anthology* (Hampshire: Isle of Wight County Press, 1951). Interestingly, Alice Meynell, who became a well-known writer and poet, was herself a convert to Catholicism.

3   For a valid baptism, it is necessary to pour water over the
    head of the candidate, and to say 'I baptise you in the name
    of the Father, the Son and the Holy Spirit', and there was
    concern that not all Anglicans did this.
4   *Bulmer's History and Directory of Cumberland* (Cumberland:
    Bulmer and Co, 1901).
5   *The London Gazette* (25 November 1910).

CHAPTER THREE

 IRGITTA IS SWEDEN'S most famous saint, and one who for centuries defined and inspired her country's sense of identity. She was born in 1303, the daughter of Birger Persson, the Governor Uppland. They were one of the richest and most important families in the country, and through her mother, who came from the Folkunda family, she was also directly related to the Swedish kings.

In 1316, when she was 13, Birgitta married the nobleman Ulf Gudmarsson, creating an alliance of great importance. It was understood that their life would be connected to that of the royal throne of Sweden and to the political, social, and military life of the nation at its very heart.

Birgitta and Ulf had eight children, four daughters and four sons. Birgitta was extremely devoted to the Church, and this had a profound influence on her husband and children. One of her daughters, Catherine, would later follow her into religious life. In 1341 Birgitta and her husband went on a lengthy pilgrimage to the great shrine at Santiago de Compostella in Spain, returning two years later. The following year Ulf, who had gone to stay in a Cistercian monastery, Alvastra Abbey in Oestergoetland, died. The widowed Birgitta then herself took religious vows, establishing the Order of the Holy Saviour. These nuns would become known as Bridgettines. Their mother house was established at Vadstena and the King, Magnus Eriksson and his queen endowed it and gave it royal status.

But the primary importance of Birgitta came from her mysticism. She spoke about visions she had had from childhood onwards, of Christ, his nativity, his passion and death. The way she described the birth of Christ—the baby lying naked on the floor, with light shining from him, and Mary and Joseph kneeling in adoration—had a profound effect as her visions were widely publicised. They came to affect religious art, and to create a standard image of the Nativity scene as it would be depicted for generations.

Birgitta became well known in Rome, where she went in 1350 initially to obtain from the Pope the authorisation for her new religious order. She made the city her home for twenty years, establishing a convent near Campo de Fiori in the city centre and working among the poor and sick. She became immensely popular and well-loved. She made a lengthy pilgrimage to Jerusalem, but otherwise remained in Rome and in 1370 her new Order had its rule confirmed: it would for the next centuries play a major role in the life of the Church. She died in 1373 and was initially buried in Rome, but her body was later brought back to Sweden. In 1391 she was canonised as a saint by Pope Boniface IX. Her daughter Catherine was also later canonised—a rare example of a mother and daughter both formally acknowledged as saints.

Birgitta's life, her mysticism, and her visions, made her a central figure of the early Middle Ages. Her Order was to become bound up with concepts of chivalry and the chivalric ideal—the nobility at the service of the poor and sick, and royalty as something to be associated with sacrifice, duty, and support for the Church. In Scandinavia, it was instrumental in nurturing education and spreading literacy and culture. Birgitta's daughter Catherine was a leading figure in the mother house at Vadstena. In due course there would be some 80 Bridgettine houses across Europe.

The Bridgettines were an order for both men and women. At each convent, there was a group of canons to be the chaplains—but all under the overall direction of a lady abbess. The special devotion of the Order was to the passion of Christ, and all the nuns wore—and still wear—an unusual head-dress over their veils, in the form of a cross, with five small red marks to signify Christ's five wounds.[1]

In England a Bridgettine convent of was established at Syon Abbey in Isleworth, Middlesex on the banks of the Thames. It was endowed by King Henry V in 1415 and was one of the most important religious centres of the country.

Then in the 16th century, tragedy struck with Henry VIII's forcible closure of all the abbeys, convents and monasteries across Britain. Syon Abbey, along with so many others, was destroyed. Although briefly restored under Queen Mary, the nuns were finally forced to flee in the reign of Elizabeth, establishing themselves initially in the Low Countries and in France, before settling in Portugal. In the 19th century the Bridgettine Order returned to Britain, its members proud of an unbroken link which bound them to their origins at Syon House.

In the early 20th century, Father Benedict Williamson, a priest working at Earlsfield in South London, with a passionate interest in the chivalric ideas, art and architecture of the Middle Ages, committed himself to a restoration of the Bridgettine Order.

Williamson, born in 1868, studied law and then trained as an architect with the firm of Newman and Jacques in Stratford in East London. In 1896 he became a Catholic at Farm Street Jesuit church in London, taking the baptismal name of Benedict, by which he was then afterwards always known. His faith and his architectural work were bound closely together: in his first years after qualifying he worked on part of the Abbey at Farnborough in Hampshire (founded by the exiled Empress Eugenie of France) and on the impressive church of St Ignatius at Stamford Hill in London. In 1906 he went to Rome to study for the priesthood at the Beda College, and was ordained in 1909.

Father Benedict was something of a romantic historian, as well as a practical man of many gifts. As a priest, he was given the charge of what was then known as St Gregory's Mission at Earlsfield. This was — and is — a busy suburb on the outskirts of Wimbledon, and there was plenty of work for him to do with a growing Catholic congregation. But he also continued to work as an architect. Working with J. H. Beart Foss of Ealing, he drew up plans and designs for a number of Catholic churches. He had a great knowledge of ecclesiastical architecture and considerable talent.

The chivalric and Medieval origins of the Bridgettines deeply attracted Fr Benedict, and he felt himself called to revive the male branch of the Order. In 1905 he met Sister Elisabeth Hesselblad, the remarkable Swedish woman, a convert from the Lutheran church, who had worked to re-establish the original house of St Birgitta in Rome. Sister Elisabeth — of whom more later — had emigrated from her native Sweden to America as a young woman, and after working for

some years as a nurse had become a Catholic and felt
called to the religious life and specifically, and power-
fully, to become a Bridgettine and to revive the Order
which had been founded in Sweden so many centuries
before. She felt a great sense of unity with St Birgitta
and her mission, and in this had a real soul-mate in
Father Benedict. As Sister Elisabeth's biographer notes:

> It was an integral part of Birgitta's plan for her
> Order that it was to consist of nuns and brothers
> (*fraters*) who should be the priests and counsel-
> lors of the Sisters. This had proved to be a sound
> concept, and was no doubt one of the reasons
> that the Order spread and developed so suc-
> cessfully during the Middle Ages. Of the twen-
> ty-seven convents of that time, all were
> balanced by the presence of brothers, who
> shared large churches with the cloistered Sis-
> ters. The Sisters usually had a choir high up in
> the apse of the church, while the brothers who
> were also, for the most part priests, officiated
> and sang close to the altar. Once a day choirs
> chanted the verses of the *Ave Maria Stella* back
> and forth together, making a marvellous music,
> in the vast stone buildings.
>
> Anyone as artistic as Father Benedict must have
> relished this thought and dreamt of a day when
> such communities might be revived.[2]

Something of the passion with which Fr Benedict took
up the cause can be seen in the letter that he sent round
to friends and supporters in 1912:

> The work is one that should appeal in a very
> special way to all those who long for the con-
> version of our fellow-countrymen to the Catho-
> lic Faith, because the Order is one of those links

> that unite the present to the past. Alone amongst all the communities that flourished before the Reformation our Sisters of Syon Abbey have maintained unbroken their community life through the nearly three hundred and fifty years that have passed since that time... The work of reviving the Fathers of the Order has possessed from the first the generous sympathy, help, and prayers of our sisters at Syon, as well as all the existing communities abroad, especially those in Spain and Germany...[3]

His first work had been to enlarge the modest church at Earlsfield, and this he did to good effect, doubling its size and adding a sacristy. He wanted to make it a real centre of religious life, and so in addition to daily Mass and confessions he established the nightly singing of Compline, followed by Benediction. This seems to have been quite well attended, with people making the effort to come in spite of their work and home duties. In those pre-television days, weekday evening activities at church were a feature of life for people of all Christian denominations in Britain.

> A large number of converts have been received into the Church, and there are at the present moment a larger number under instruction than at any period since we have had charge of the Mission. The Children are instructed in the Catechism on four days each week, so as to supply the lack of a Catholic School. The Congregation has more than doubled during the past two years, and is constantly increasing, and indeed the work in Earlsfield promises to be very fruitful indeed.[4]

He suggested that a circle of supporters be established, each contributing £1 towards the work of the Earlsfield church or to helping students who were considering joining the revived Bridgettines and were currently in various colleges preparing to enter the Novitiate. It was an ambitious project, as the work of St Gregory's parish alone was enough to keep him busy. But he was attracting men to join the Bridgettines, emphasising the value of community life and the special character of an Order that had its origins in the days of a Catholic Europe. And he talked to people in the parish about the Bridgettines and his ideas for participating in the revival of this Order. Among them was the Flanagan family, and they form the next chapter of this story.

Notes

1   For this reason, they are sometimes known as the 'hot cross bun nuns'!

2   M. Tjader, *The Most Extraordinary Woman in Rome* (Rome: Generalate House, Sisters of St Bridget, 1987), p. 83–84.

3   *Our Saviour's Messenger*, 1912, Archives of RC diocese of Southwark.

4   *Ibid.*

CHAPTER FOUR

HE FLANAGANS WERE a devout Irish family—William John Flangan, a solicitor's clerk, married to Florence Emily, nee Murray. Their daughter Florence Katherine, known as Kitty or Kate, was born on 17 July 1892, and baptised at St Peter's, Clerkenwell, the Catholic chapel in London's Hatton Garden.[1] The family lived at number 37, Durnsford Avenue, Wimbledon Park. Kitty was their oldest child, and would in due course be followed by two boys, George and Francis, and another girl, Dorothy. Kitty was confirmed in 1904 at St Boniface's church in Tooting—St Gregory's did not open until November of that year.

In a memoir of Katherine Flanagan, written anonymously by a Bridgettine sister—almost certainly Mother Riccarda—in 1941, very much in the religious style of its day, we learn that 'She was reared in a home where the whole atmosphere was definitely Catholic, and in those surroundings the children learned to love their religion, and what is more to live it. In Lent and Advent they were accustomed to offer their little sacrifices to Jesus. Mass was never missed on Sundays or Holidays, there was no foolish indulgence, especially at table, and thus children always received gratefully that which was set before them. In this home at once affectionate and austere, little Katherine early began to feel the call of the Lord to a complete dedication of herself to Him'.[2] Katherine would later recall a

very happy childhood, and liked to sing her father's
favourite hymn:

> O Jesus Christ remember
> When thou shalt come again
> Upon the clouds of Heaven
> With all Thy shining train.[3]

As a young woman, working as a dressmaker, Katherine Flanagan came regularly to the singing of Compline at St Gregory's church, and it was this that seems
to have fostered her religious vocation. Fr Benedict
would later write 'The Choral Worship brings out the
meaning of the Liturgy in a way that no private
recitation possibly can. Mother Katherine first acquired
this love of the Divine Office in our parish of St
Gregory where a a young girl she rarely missed the
Office of Compline sung every night in the Church,
where the whole Congregation took their part in the
Liturgy. I well remember, how after she had become
a Bridgettine nun she spoke on the subject of Choral
Worship and how careful she was that nothing should
be wanting in the perfection with which it was
performed….And this daily round of praise and
adoration holds a high place in the life of the Bridgettine nun, for round it revolves all the other activities
of the Order. The Psalter of David with its one hundred
and fifty Psalms form the body of this Worship embroi-
dered with antiphons, hymns, responsories, lessons
and canticles all fitly joined together to make one
perfect whole. And the birth, life, Passion, death,
resurrection and Ascension form the principle theme
for the circling year, while scattered through it come
the feasts of the Blessed Virgin and the Saints like
jewels upon a golden crown…'[4]

Fr Benedict clearly had a great enthusiasm for the chanted Offices of the Church, and especially of the Bridgettine Order. But he found it was no easy matter to combine the re-establishment of a religious order with the busy life of a parish. His novices who joined with great enthusiasm found that the project did not really work, despite energetic efforts, and they did not stay. His original plan was to move from St Gregory's to a proper monastery but when a lack of numbers made this impractical he started things at Earlsfield, noting in his *Our Saviour's Messenger* newsletter the plan to develop the buildings there to include rooms for novices. He started a group of Oblates, drawing up statues for them so that they were properly established and linking them to the community of nuns at Syon. Some fifty people joined this group, living and working as usual in their everyday lives, but being associated with the Bridgettine way of life in prayer and gathering for retreats and spiritual conferences from time to time. But getting novices for the Order was another matter. Some young men joined in 1912 but by the following year had left again.

Kitty Flanagan, however, felt a real call to the life of the Bridgettines. It is clear that Fr Benedict had inspired her with his descriptions of the Medieval communities, their music, their culture, their achieve-ments. She was prepared to take the great step of leaving her family, travelling to Rome, and embarking on this wholly new way of life. This did not mean joining an already thriving community, but helping to establish one. Mother Elisabeth Hesselblad was in the process of founding a Bridgettine house in Rome but had faced huge difficulties in obtaining the premises—the original house of St Birgitta—and in making any

progress in bringing together a community there. Kitty
Flanagan would be leaving her home for something
that was a wholly new project, albeit one with very
ancient foundations.

This was an extraordinary step for a young woman
in 1909. The journey itself—no simple flight in a plane
in the 1900s, but a complicated trip by road and rail
across Europe and through the Alps—was a major
undertaking. Nor would there be any easy return. The
decision to enter religious life was not a light one, and
although it was of course possible to leave the Order
in the early years before Final Vows were taken, it was
not something easily done, as it entailed making
entirely fresh plans for a future life with no funds and
no support, with no professional qualifications and at
a time when career opportunities for women were
limited.

In addition, Kitty Flanagan was extremely close to
her parents and family, and did not want to leave
them. She was well aware that the chances of them
coming to visit her in Rome were minimal—the family
was not well-off and European travel was not something they ever contemplated.

In 1911, she made up her mind. She was not alone
in her decision—another local girl, Amy Davies, was
also keen to join the Bridgettines, and they would
travel with Fr Benedict to the Mother House in Rome,
the house where St Bridget herself had lived, and start
as novices there. It was a dramatic and radical step. Fr
Benedict must have felt that all his prayers and all his
disappointments had at least had this outcome—some
girls from England were going to Rome to be part of
what would surely be a great revival of the Bridgettines, restoring England to Catholic life and worship.

He was confident about the two girls and their future 'They both had excellent voices and ardent, spiritual natures. He had inspired them with an interest in St Birgitta and the new work which was to be a counterpart of his own'.[5] In fact, they were to succeed where he would not—although he gave a life of dedicated service to the Church, it was not as part of a Bridgettine community, as he was never able to persuade any men to join him in the project, although many expressed interest or stayed for a short period.

The little group of travellers—Fr Benedict and the prospective nuns—set off by train from Earlsfield in September 1911. It is in fact not clear if there were three girls in the group, or only two. Fr Benedict mentions three, but Amy Davies, who became Sister Reginalda, kept a diary of the days of the convent in Rome on the instructions of Mother Elisabeth Hesselblad and mentions only two, namely herself and Kate Flanagan. It seems likely that the third girl, if there was one, eventually decided not to stay with the Bridgettines, and thus leaves the story and indeed Sister Reginalda's records.

Both Kitty and Amy were by now steeped in the whole idea of the Bridgettine tradition. Kitty was pleased that she bore the same name, Katherine, as St Birgitta's daughter, who followed her mother in the Order and like her was later proclaimed a saint.

Fr Benedict writes that Katherine Flanagan was 'then a young girl of nineteen full of enthusiasm and great ideals' and the journey was evidently taken with a great sense of high purpose, every moment memorable. They made their first stop for the night at Lucerne where 'our evening meal was taken beside the lake, with the lights of the city reflected in the waters,

which imparted a fairy-like beauty to the scene.' The
next morning he celebrated Mass 'in a noble gothic
church near by, and the three girls were given places
in the handsome choir-stalls of the spacious sanctuary.'[6]
The girls were thrilled with everything they saw:

> We entered Italy through the magnificent
> scenery of the St Gothard pass, which filled the
> three girls with admiration at God's marvellous
> works; they were all the more impressed as it
> was the first time they had been out of England.

They travelled through the night and arrived very
early in Rome, going straight to the convent. There
they were met by Sister Elisabeth Hesselblad who now,
with the establishment of the community, would be
transformed from a lone Sister in Rome to the superior
of a convent, and the title of Mother.

> It was about half-past seven and she was in the
> room of St Birgitta, arranging the altar for Mass,
> when she heard the door-bell ring. On the
> threshold was Fr Benedict Williamson, with two
> English girls who became the first two postu-
> lants—Sister Katherine and Sister Reginalda.
>
> A few moments to remove the dust of the long
> journey, and they all entered the room of St
> Birgitta, where Fr Benedict said Mass and gave
> Holy Communion to the nascent Community.[7]

In recording the moment, Mother Elisabeth mentions
specifically the singing, which Fr Benedict had already
noted as being of particular importance: 'With their
good voices, they have been able to sing the praises of
Our Lord and His Blessed Mother according to the
chant of the beautiful and ancient Bridgettine Office

which now, at last, was recited once more in the Eternal City.'[8]

It is a pity that all the written records of this event are in the formal and slightly sentimental style that seemed to be felt to be required of all religious writing of the period, but even allowing for this we do get a flavour of the event, and they were in any case absolutely dedicated to doing everything in the formal and traditional Bridgettine way, so perhaps the style is appropriate. Fr Benedict evidently stayed on for some weeks to get the community life started: 'From the very first day, we had the consolation of being able to sing part of the Bridgettine Office together, and Father Benedict gave frequent instructive conferences.'[9]

Notes

[1] Now the Italian church, in the care of the Pallotine Fathers.

[2] *Mother Mary Katherine Flanagan*, by a Sister of the Order (Vatican: Tipographia Poliglotta Vaticana, 1941).

[3] *Ibid.*

[4] *Ibid*, Foreword by Fr B. Williamson.

[5] M. Tjader, *The Most Extraordinary Woman in Rome* (Rome: Generalate House, Sisters of St Bridget, 1987), p. 114.

[6] Fr B. Williamson, in a Foreword to *Mother Katherine Flanagan*, published privately by the Bridgettine sisters, undated.

[7] Sister Reginalda's diary of the Convent, quoted in Tjader, *The Most Extraordinary Woman in Rome*, p. 115.

[8] Mother Elisabeth Hesselblad, quoted in Tjader, *The Most Extraordinary Woman in Rome*, p. 115.

[9] Sister Reginalda, quoted in Tjader, *The Most Extraordinary Woman in Rome*, p. 116.

CHAPTER FIVE

HAT WAS THIS Bridgettine house that Kitty Flanagan—now Sister Katherine—had joined? Mother Elisabeth was born Maria Elisabeth Hesselblad in the village of Foglavik, in Vastergotland in Sweden on 4 June 1870. She was one of thirteen children. The family were middle-class but struggled financially. They were devout Lutherans and had been influenced by the religious revival that had occurred earlier in the 19th century when the new evangelical movements—not unlike the preaching of John Wesley in England—were making an impact. She was deeply interested in the Christian faith, and her confirmation made a great impression on her. She would also later recall an extraordinary experience in childhood when she had a vision, in what she thought was a dream, of a house where one window in particular drew her attention, and of herself subsequently in the house and looking out from it.

Along with many other Scandinavian young people at the end of the 19th century, Maria went to America in search of work, initially with families in New York as a nursemaid, studying English at night in the kitchen after days of fetching and carrying, cooking and cleaning. Ill health brought a lengthy stay in hospital and this prompted her to become a nurse herself.

It was in big public hospital in New York that she first encountered Catholicism, frequently being sent to get a priest from nearby St Patrick's Cathedral for a dying patient and being impressed with the clergy - their faith, their certainty, and the dedicated way in which they served their people. She became very friendly with a Catholic family from South America, who took her with them to Benediction and to a procession of the Blessed Sacrament. Although deeply attracted by the Eucharist, she fought against the idea of becoming a Catholic. She was upset when a friend became first a Catholic and then a nun, wondering what to make of a Church which made such huge demands on people. She would later explain that when she did eventually join the Church, it was with a great and strong conviction of being connected with the Truth.

On a trip back to Europe, arranged with her South American friends, Maria went to Sweden while they travelled to London. She was joyfully reunited with her family, and was able to spend Christmas with them, relishing the snow and the beauty of her home-land, and the familiar food and customs. But she realised that her decision to become a Catholic had caused her family some pain, and brought a break with their traditions and sense of family unity. There were tense moments when she crossed herself after praying, and arguments about priestly celibacy and about the idea of convents and monasteries. She loved Sweden, and her earnings in New York had funded a small country home for her now elderly mother, where it was evident that they could both settle happily, in surroundings that they both loved. But she felt called to something different, something more challenging and much more difficult, although uncertain what it was, and she knew she must leave.

> In the pine forest not far from our house was a
> grotto made by Nature herself at the foot of a
> small crag, and the deep snow that covered the
> forest did not come near this cave under the
> rocks. Here I used to go and pray alone... I felt
> that God wanted something of me, that I could
> not continue my life as before.[1]

The friends with whom she had travelled to Europe
took her with them to England and from there to
Rome, where she had the shock of recognising the very
house she had seen in her childhood dream. It was in
the Piazza Farnese and was the house where St Birgitta
had lived centuries before.

> The cabbie stood up and turned to explain that
> the Palazzo Farnese was a masterpiece of
> Michelangelo and Sangallo. But the words stuck
> in his mouth. He had seen many strange tour-
> ists, but this one must be crazy. She was stand-
> ing bolt upright in the carriage—white as a
> sheet—and staring across the right side of the
> square.[2]

Eventually, after many difficulties and struggles,
Maria Hesselblad was to live in that house, first as a
guest of the Carmelite sisters who at that time occupied
it, and finally as the founder, or rather re-founder, of
a Bridgettine community there. As described above,
she was eventually to welcome her first two novices
and be at Mass with them in the very room where St
Birgitta lived and worked.

Mother Elisabeth Hesselblad—she took the name
Elisabeth when making her religious vows - was a
woman of immense vigour, faith, and determination.
Her re-establishment of the Bridgettine Order brought
her eventually into contact with Bishops, members of

the Swedish Royal Family and Popes. But the early days were extremely difficult, and the small community of women lived in real poverty, dependent on gifts from others. Her health had never been good since the days in New York when some mismanaged hospital treatment had caused stomach problems that were to be lifelong. The use of St Birgitta's house was initially only temporary, and there were tensions with the Carmelite community. There was also no money for her small community, and uncertainty about its future.

This was the position when Fr Benedict arrived from London with the two girls, Kitty Flanagan and Amy Davies.

Kitty Flanagan did not find her first year in Rome easy. She was extremely homesick:

> intensely affectionate as she was, she had to wage a hard battle during the first year of her convent life, for her thoughts constantly turned to her father to whom she was so passionately attached, indeed her separation from him was perhaps the greatest sacrifice of her life.[3]

Another young woman, Agnes Lincoln—a niece of the famous American president—joined the community at about this time, and would later be sponsor to Kitty Flanagan when she made her first vows. Ill health, however, prevented Agnes from making her own full vows alongside and sadly she was to die not very long afterwards.

Then in 1912, a year after the arrival of Katherine Flanagan and Amy Davies, Madeleine Hambrough arrived in Rome. Unlike the first two girls, she had not been brought up in Fr Benedict Williamson's parish, and must have met him at some stage after leaving school. As no one else was promoting the Bridgettines in England at that time, it was certainly under his influence that she came to hear about them and about the work of Mother Elisabeth. Her own life had reached a crossroads in 1911 with her father's death, and her decision to leave Britain and journey to Rome to start a wholly new life of commitment as a Bridgettine nun was made in the wake of this. So far as is known, she was never to see her mother again: although they would presumably have corresponded, the journey to Rome would have been arduous and complicated, and in any case the First World War was shortly to intervene. Her older brother Dudley died in 1926 and Mrs Hambrough died in 1927, living in Putney, South London. Madeleine's other brother, Basil, of whom more later, went on to have a distinguished military career and later to settle in Kenya.

Madeleine had come to Rome at a difficult time for the small new Bridgettine community—Mother Elisabeth was ill, and the community had to leave St Birgitta's house as the Carmelites required the rooms. In August, another house was found for them, number 113 on the Via Aurelia, though it was in a state of very poor repair. Its one advantage was that it overlooked St Peter's Basilica. As it had no chapel, the sisters went to St Peter's for daily Mass. They worked hard to make the building habitable, and moved in on 17 December . Later that month, Mother Elisabeth had an audience of the Pope, Pius X, and the following June he signed the necessary documents that formally brought the revived Bridgettine Order into existence.

Madeleine Hambrough was clearly a young woman of definite and strong convictions. It was normal to choose a new name on entering a religious order, and she chose that of a male saint, Richard Reynolds. It was her third change of name, and she was still in her early twenties. The name was chosen to honour the English Martyr, Richard Reynolds. He was a Bridgettine monk, executed — by being hanged, drawn, and quartered — in 1535 under Henry VIII for refusing to sign the Act of Supremacy which affirmed the King as head of the Church of England. He was thus a contemporary of Saints John Fisher and Thomas More, and died as they did for the principle of the union of the Church with the successor of St Peter. Richard Reynolds was one of the Forty English Martyrs canonised by Pope Paul VI in 1970, but back in 1912 he was not formally a saint in the Catholic Church. Choosing him as her patron in the religious life was a statement of commitment to the unbroken Bridgettine tradition and to the conversion of England, the unity of the Church in her native country with that of the Church worldwide.

Living in Rome, the community naturally spoke Italian, and thus although Madeleine was to be known as Mother Richard in the English form, she was frequently and more usually known by the feminised and Italian form of the name, Riccarda.

Thus, by the summer of 1913, a year and a half after they had first arrived in Rome, Kate Flanagan and Amy Davies, now officially Sister Katherine and Sister Reginalda, were wearing the white veils of the noviti-ate along with Agnes Lincoln , now Sister Agnes, and Sister Riccarda, formerly Madeleine Hambrough. All were wearing the Bridgettine head-dress, with its five red dots honouring the five wounds of Christ, and the Bridgettine grey habit with its long loose folds. After much worry and struggle, the Bridgettine Order had been re-established in Rome.

This small Bridgettine community in Rome had been brought together by a Swedish woman to revive a religious order with Swedish roots. Elisabeth Hesselblad's own experience of being brought up in a Lutheran tradition meant that she understood the English situation very well, and had much in common with an English Catholic from a convert background such as Sister Riccarda Hambrough.

Back in England, Fr Benedict was still busy hoping to establish a men's section of the Order. But the events of the next years were to see the final ending to those plans. He moved to Cobham in Surrey and initially plans for a Bridgettine novitiate there seemed to prosper. But it was 1914 and war intervened. He volunteered to serve as a chaplain. Priests were needed in the front line with the young soldiers of the British Army who were facing death. In due course he would serve on the Western front, wrecking his health in the process, following gas attacks.[4]

In Rome, war meant that the young members of the small Bridgettine community were now cut off from their families not only by distance and by commitment to a religious community which restricted travel and bound them to a fixed rule of life, but also by the battle lines. They had little news from their families. Sister Riccarda's brother Basil had transferred from the Norfolk Regiment to the Welsh Guards on the outbreak of war. It was to be the start of a distinguished military career: he would in due course serve with a Cossack regiment and later go on to achieve the rank of Lieutenant Colonel. Meanwhile the sisters in Rome would soon find that they had plenty of work to do.

Notes

1   Mother Elisabeth Hesselblad, in *The Most Extraordinary Woman in Rome*, by M. Tjader (Rome: Generalate House, Sisters of St Bridget, 1987) p. 37.

2   Tjader *The Most Extraordinary Woman in Rome*, p. 40.

3   *Mother Mary Katherine Flanagan*, By a Sister of the Order (Vatican: Tipographia Poliglotta Vaticana, 1941).

4   Nicknamed 'Happy' he became a popular chaplain, serving with great courage, and would later publish his wartime memories under the surely somewhat ironic title of 'Happy days in Flanders'.

CHAPTER SIX

 N JANUARY 1915 a massive earthquake hit Italy. It would turn out to be one of the worst the country had ever know. Some 30,000 people were killed, and whole towns and villages were swept away. Huge numbers of people were wounded. The town of Avezzano, at the epicentre of the quake, was completely obliterated.

The quake was felt in Rome, and the Sisters, who were singing the office of Sext when it occurred, felt the room sway around them. One would later remember the sanctuary lamp swinging randomly. All felt sick and giddy.

With Europe at war, and basic supplies of all kinds in short supply, the plight of the victims of the earthquake was bleak. Many were brought to Rome. The Bridgettine sisters were asked if they could take in some of the orphaned children and naturally opened their doors at once. Six little girls arrived, each one with a grim story to tell. None of them had parents any more.

> One had lain for four hours under stones and debris, before she was rescued. Her mother died before her eyes. Another had her little brother, five months old, in her arms when the shock came: the baby was crushed but she escaped with slight injuries.[1]

Just as they were coping with all of this, and making a home for the children in their convent, they received news that they must leave. The landlord was putting up the rent, and they could no longer afford to remain there. Mother Elisabeth was able to find another house, on the Via Corsica—in the ordinary way it would have been too large for their needs but now with the orphans they needed the extra space, and indeed would be able to welcome more children.

It was to prove a busy summer, and funds were always low so that giving the children everything they needed required ingenuity and sacrifice.

It was just at this time that permission was received for the novices to make their formal profession as nuns, exchanging the white veils they had worn as novices for black ones. Sister Agnes was no longer with them, but a Sister Birgitta had joined them. They made a retreat with a French priest, Father Hattais, who had become the convent's chaplain, and on 8 September—the feast of the Birthday of Our Lady—the ceremony took place. The following year two Italian girls joined them, Sisters Raffaela and Michaela, and in 1916 came the first Swedish novice, Sister Elena. By 1917, when Cardinal Bourne, the Archbishop of Westminster, was able to visit from England, the community was ten in number.

During the war years the Sisters main work was in caring for orphaned and wounded children, the victims of the earthquake and also of the war. They took in badly injured people following the battle of Caporetto, stretching their accommodation almost to breaking point, but reluctant to turn anyone away. Italy's losses in the battle were huge—11,000 were killed and some 20,000 were wounded. In the aftermath there were many deserters. Italy, like all the other nations of Europe, was seeing human suffering on an enormous scale.

Meanwhile, Riccarda was hearing news from home. Her brother Basil, serving with the Welsh Guards, had gone out to France in August 1915 with the British Expeditionary Force, having been promoted to the rank of Lieutenant in June of that year. On 18 October 1915 he was badly wounded and invalided home to England. It was of course not possible for his sister to travel from Italy to be with him, and she simply had to wait for letters with news. Earlier during the battle of Loos, he had had a narrow escape when sitting with some bombs in a cellar. The house was hit, a shell penetrating the cellar—a corporal, Davies, was killed but Hambrough and a friend, Charles Greville from the Grenadier Guards, escaped unharmed.[2]

By the end of 1915, of the thirty officers with whom Hambrough had travelled out to France only eleven were left. He recovered from his wounds and the following year was sent out once again to the trenches, serving in France from June 1916 to January 1917 when he became ill and again had to be shipped back to England. He then served as adjutant in the Welsh Guards in the final year of the war, being promoted to the rank of Captain in June 1918.

Basil Hambrough would go on to have an extraordinary life. He is mentioned in the autobiography of novelist Anthony Powell, where he is described as being in appearance a 'typical guardsman, brushed-up moustache, brigade tie…' but with an unconventional lifestyle. He also features in some of Powell's novels in the characters of Dicky Umfraville and Eustace Bromwell.[3] He had innumerable adventures which included being assistant military attaché in Greece, being awarded the OBE, and running a farm in Africa, and was married a total of four times. His final mar-

riage was to Monica Nickalls with whom he moved to
Kenya and had a family—of whom more later.

At the end of the First World War, the Bridgettine
Sisters in Rome faced another move—the lease was up
on the premises at the Villa Corsica, where they had
now been for three years. The local people of the
district did not want them to leave and sent a large
delegation to say so. Providentially, a property became
vacant just next door and seemed ideal, but the sisters
had no funds. Mother Elisabeth appealed directly the
Pope, Benedict XV, who showed great interest. It was,
after all, most unusual to have an Order in Rome
headed by a Scandinavian and with a special devotion
to St Birgitta. He asked to see Mother Elisabeth and
she spoke to him about the work the sisters were
doing. Funds became available on a loan—which the
sisters were able in the event to pay off after five years.
In April 1919 the sisters moved to their new home,
which they were to occupy for twelve years. They
celebrated with Adoration of the Blessed Sacrament in
the chapel all day, ending with Benediction at 5pm and
a big tea-party. A number of diplomats from the
various Scandinavian countries attended, and the
various Scandinavian flags had been arranged around
a statue of the Virgin Mary in the parlour.

What were they like, these sisters living the Bridgettine way of life, conscious of having revived a
tradition that had its origins in the early Middle Ages?
The community had now, with sisters from Sweden,
England and Italy, in a sense, come of age. It had its
own traditions and atmosphere. There was a strong
commitment to the idea of restoring the Catholic faith
to Scandinavia, and of giving back to the people of
Sweden a real sense of the heritage that was theirs

through St Birgitta. There was a zeal in living the community life—singing the Office together, holding all things in common, keeping the vows of poverty, chastity and obedience which are at the core of this religious commitment.

St Birgitta had not founded her religious order to do any one specific work—it was not dedicated solely to any one project such as founding schools or hospitals or ministering to the poor. The Bridgettine idea was to live the full evangelical life and be responsive to whatever needs emerged. Thus the sisters cared for the victims of earthquake and war, and also provided hospitality for visitors to Rome. But they also always saw the house in Rome as being at the centre of a Bridgettine revival elsewhere—they looked to Britain and to Scandinavia in particular. The idea would be to establish houses which would evangelise and spread the message of the Church simply through the witness of a Bridgettine way of life—the attraction of prayer, especially the beauty of the Office sung together, and of a community bound by charity, good work, and a common faith. The actual work to be done would vary from place to place—a retreat centre, a guest-house, care of refugees—but the core of the Bridgettine vocation was prayer, and they believed that by living according to the Bridgettine rule with its daily sung Offices they were doing something of value.

The young women who had come from England seem to have adapted with enthusiasm and zeal to the Bridgettine way as taught by Mother Elisabeth and Father Benedict. It was not an easy way. The notion of holding all things in common was upheld strictly. They used the expression "our" rather than "my" for all everyday objects such as a pen, a spoon, a piece of

kitchen equipment, even the grey Bridgettine habits
that they wore, so as not to show any desire for
personal ownership of any kind. A small incident
reveals this: in her early days in Rome, Sister Katherine
Flanagan took on the task of refilling small oil lamps
from another sister, who was taller. The other sister
did not need to stand on a chair to do this task, and
Sister Katherine attempted to do it in the same way,
but failed, and the oil splashed down the front of her
new Bridgettine robes. She rushed to Mother Elisabeth
and said 'Mea culpa—I have ruined our new habit'.
She also drew a moral lesson from the incident, using
the analogy between accepting the fact of not being
tall, and accepting the need to remain humble—one
should never seek to be "high" in any way.[4] Perhaps
all this sounds a bit pious and sanctimonious—but it
reveals a genuine desire to live according to the
strictest rules, even at the risk of being a little scrupu-
lous.

But they did enjoy celebrating together, and took
care to make arrangements for feast-days and special
anniversaries. There was pride in the Scandinavian
links and, as we have seen, good contacts were established with the representatives in Rome of Scandinavian nations. This was no small achievement: tensions
between the Catholic Church and the Protestant
nations of Northern Europe had been tense since the
Reformation, some 400 years earlier. Breaking that ice
would take time—there were many misunderstand-
ings and difficulties to overcome.

The year 1923 would mark the 550th anniversary of
St Birgitta's death, and events were being planned in
Sweden. There had been a revival of interest in her,
and old anti-Catholic prejudices were fading. 'A group

of distinguished Swedish friends of Birgitta, most of them High Church Lutherans, led by Count and Countess von Rosen and encouraged by Bishop Nathan Soederblom and other churchmen, had founded a *Societas Sancta Birgittae*, using the Latin name which connotated their historical interest and the fact that they admired classic liturgy. They had determined to gather each year at Vadstena on the anniversary of Birgitta's death, and to honour her by wearing gray Bridgettine robes for this occasion, marching in procession to the old convent church, where medieval singing and ceremonies emulating those of Birgitta's day were held.'[5] Count and Countess von Rosen now invited Mother Elisabeth, accompanied by another sister, to visit Sweden for this special anniversary as their guest.

The ceremonies in Vadstena included Bridgettine chanting, and the laying of wreaths at the tomb of St Birgitta in the famous Blue Church, led by Prince Eugene of Sweden. Some two thousand people crammed into the church, with many more thronging outside.

The Swedish trip also brought a great development—working with Bishop Muller, Mother Elisabeth acquired a property at Djursholm, a suburb of Stockholm, where she planned to established 'St Birgitta's Vilohem', St Birgitta's Rest Home—a place of welcome for anyone, where people could come and stay, pray, relax, and receive the hospitality of the sisters.

Back in Rome, Sister Katherine Flanagan had been left in charge. Mother Elisabeth wrote to tell her of the plans for Djursholm. There were some local prejudices to overcome—the people of the neighbourhood knew little or nothing about Catholicism and some believed it to be associated with black magic and evil things.

But gradually this changed, and by October, when the house was formally opened by Bishop Muller, there was much friendliness from many of their neighbours.

Sister Riccarda travelled from Rome to help establish things at Djursholm accompanied by Sister Margherita. For Riccarda, it was the first lengthy journey since her arrival in Rome almost ten years earlier. The young woman who had arrived from England was now in her thirties. Descriptions of her comment on her unusual beauty, and she was tall. She had the look and presence of an English aristocrat, and although she now spoke Italian as a matter of course she never forgot that she was anything other than English. For the journey through Sweden, she and Sister Margherita covered their unusual Bridgettine head-dresses with black veils so as to look a little less conspicuous.

Riccarda had been brought up by her convert parents to have a strong belief in the importance of restoring Catholicism to lands that had been cut off from Rome at the Reformation, and so for her the establishment of Djursholm would have been of immense symbolic significance. The team of nuns worked hard to make the house a place of welcome. Mother Elisabeth's family donated furniture and other items. A priest came out from Stockholm daily to celebrate Mass, and a small group of Oblates was formed—rather like the group that Fr Benedict Williamson had formed in London many years before.

Djursholm became immensely popular. Within months of its opening, it was oversubscribed with guests, and had a waiting list. The writer Sigrid Unset, a convert to Catholicism, was among the visitors. People loved the traditional Swedish food and hospitality, in a beautiful setting, with Catholic faith and worship. All of this involved a good deal of work—and also attracted media publicity. Articles appeared in the Swedish press about the nuns, mostly favourable and noting the historic link with St Birgitta.

In September 1924, with Djursholm established, the Bridgettines took on a new project—the opening of a house at Lugano in Switzerland. Here, by the lakeside, a house that had once belonged to an opera-singer was transformed into a convent and guest-house.

The Bridgettine Order was expanding, and would continue to do so throughout the 1920s and 30s. While Mother Elisabeth and Sister Riccarda were away in Djursholm and Lugano, Katherine Flanagan was in charge back in Rome. This was a considerable responsibility as the future of the house was always uncertain—there had already been several moves, as we have seen, because of rent rises or other sudden problems—and the role of the community in serving the needs of Scandinavian Catholics visiting Rome was expanding all the time. Sister Katherine—who, it will be recalled, had joined the order at the end of her teens, having worked as a dressmaker after leaving school—had had to learn about the management of a substantial property which catered for varying numbers of guests and visitors and which was beginning to play a significant role in the growing diplomatic exchanges between the Scandinavian representatives in Rome and the Church authorities.

Sister Katherine was in due course was given charge of the house at Lugano. She was there when, in 1931, the Bridgettines were suddenly presented with a house in England—owned by Marie Cisneros Potter, the South American friend who had first introduced Mother Elisabeth Hesselblad to the Catholic Church.

Marie Cisneros had married, late in life, an eccentric Englishman Norman Potter[6] who had originally been running a Catholic boys' home in Clapham Park in South London. They were now spending most of their time abroad, and she donated the house they owned at Iver Heath near Uxbridge to the Bridgettines. Sister Katherine Flanagan was sent from Lugano to England to take charge of this new property and create a full Bridgettine community there. She did this with immense vigour and success, building a chapel on to the side of the property and some extra rooms for the nuns. Local Catholics, who had no place of worship nearby, started to arrive for Mass and over the next few years the chapel had to be expanded three times. A number of girls also came forward to join the community.

Katherine Flanagan had not seen her own family for some twenty years. While she was in Rome, they had emigrated to Australia. Both her brothers were to remain there, having found good jobs. Her parents, however, returned to England in late middle-age, and she had a great reunion with them at Iver. They became regular visitors there, attending Mass in the chapel and spending time with their daughter, now a much-honoured Mother Superior.

Mother Katherine, as we should now call her, became a well-known local figure. She was popular for her cheerfulness and kindness, and this won over people who might otherwise have been wary of Catholic nuns. In 1935 she was again summoned to new duties—a house was being established at Vadstena in Sweden, and this was to be of huge significance because it was of course the place where St Birgitta had made her first community. Mother Katherine was appointed prioress and would devote the rest of her life to it.

The Vadstena house was near Lake Vettern in the old town, and not far from the Blue Church where St Birgitta was honoured and where the big celebrations had been held in 1923 to mark her anniversary. With the opening of the new convent, the weekly newspaper *Vecko-Journalen* published a friendly welcome to the nuns: 'once more, Vadstena's narrow cobble-stoned streets will be adorned with gentle, silent Birgitta nuns who, with their habits, will set a new—or rather a medieval—stamp on the old monastery town'.[7] The opening of the house—which was to be a retreat centre, offering a welcome for those who sought spiritual renewal, or simply wanted a place to rest and be quiet for a few days—became a major public event, with an open-air Mass, a big feature interview with Mother Elisabeth in the newspaper, and a great gathering of many friends and supporters.

Mother Katherine evidently loved Vadstena. At Christmas 1935 she wrote to Mother Elisabeth in Rome

> Now the leaves have all fallen from the trees— the ground is covered with a soft blanket of pure white snow—through the trees one can see the delicate spire of the Church—the ancient Bridgettine Church—the trees are covered with rimfrost and the branches glittering as if they were set with diamonds.[8]

She speculated that she might one day lie beneath snow in the shadow of that church, and this indeed was to happen when she died in 1941 and was buried there, in a plot given to the nuns by Count and Countess von Rosen, who wanted the Bridgettines to

have a tiny bit of land associated directly with St
Birgitta herself.

Vadstena became a place where Catholic writers
and intellectuals gathered. The writer Danish Johannes
Joergensen lived there while working on a biography
of St Birgitta, and later described the pleasure of sitting
in his study near the chapel and hearing 'the clear
voices ...singing Birgitta's hymns, *Ave maris stella* and
Rosa rorans bonitatem'. Lake Vettern was known as the
'Troll-Sjo', or troll-water, because of its brisk, decep-
tive, and sometimes dangerous waves that appeared
to dance gleefully, and were never still. Jorgensen
wrote of the beauty of the winter, looking out when
'the sleepless waters of the Troll-Sjo were bound by
frost, out across the white desert of ice towards the
coast of the Vastorgotland...'[9]

Organising the Vadstena house was a very considerable task. It was meant to be a Rest Home, a place of
quietness and refreshment, and to achieve this it was
necessary to keep everything running smoothly. There
was a small gardener's cottage in the grounds which
was converted into a house for a chaplain, and many
other priests also came to stay. Guests could rest, relax,
and pray—and some liked to hear Mother Katherine
talk about St Birgitta or, in particular, about the
traditions of the Office and its music, on which she was
extremely knowledgeable. The house grew more and
more popular.

In the spring of 1939 Mother Katherine wrote very
happily to Mother Elisabeth in Rome

> I have had a letter from father and mother. They
> say they are coming to visit me: they are coming
> on a slow freight steamer, because as you know
> they have very little money, but I am pleased

they can have a nice rest while at sea, especially my father who can have a rest from his office. I am, also glad because they will see what a beautiful country Sweden is and what nice people the Swedish people are.

The visit was planned for the summer, and the Flanagan family were looking forward to a happy gathering at Vadstena with its lake and its traditions and history. But in the summer of 1939 all such pleasure trips by ordinary English families were cancelled. It was clear that another war was looming.

Notes

1   M. Tjader *The Most Extraordinary Woman in Rome* (Rome: Generalate House, Sisters of St Bridget, 1987) p. 122.

2   C. H. Dudley Ward *History of the Welsh Guards* (London: John Murray, 1920). On Internet at: www26.us.archive.org/stream/historyofwelshgu00dudl

3   A. Powell *To Keep the Ball Rolling—The memoirs of Anthony Powell* (Chicago: University of Chicago Press, 2001). For this information I am indebted to Fiona Mercey, who researched the life of Basil Hambrough and discovered the Powell references.

4   *Mother Mary Katherine Flanagan*, By a Sister of the Order (Vatican: Tipographia Poliglotta Vaticana 1941).

5   Tjader *The Most Extraordinary Woman in Rome*, p. 140.

6   Norman Potter had initiated several projects at Clapham Park in the 1900s, including a sanatorium for sick children and a boys' home, and had also personally adopted a large number of boys, giving them all his own surname. However, at one stage some of these made allegations of abuse against him, and although these were never proved it meant that he had to leave the district—he had by this time married Marie Cisneros and they moved to Switzerland where he ran a holiday scheme for boys from English schools. Some of the boys he had adopted later died in the First World War, but others—there some 60 in all—went on to marry and have

homes and families of their own. Many remembered him with great affection and regarded the abuse allegations as wholly untrue and scurrilous. After his death, Marie Potter spent much of her time at Iver Heath in the late 1930s, effectively living with the nuns. See *One Corner of London* (Leominster: Gracewing Books, 1998).

7   Quoted in Tjader, *The Most Extraordinary Woman in Rome*, p. 183.

8   *Mother Mary Katherine Flanagan*, By a Sister of the Order (Vatican: Tipographia Poliglotta Vaticana 1941).

9   Quoted in Tjader *The Most Extraordinary Woman in Rome*.

CHAPTER SEVEN

HE BRIDGETTINE HOUSE in Rome had an early clash with Mussolini's fascist regime, thanks to an almost absurd incident involving an Irish woman visitor. Mussolini came to power in 1925, and one afternoon in the April of the following year a group of policemen suddenly arrived at the house demanding entrance. They asked to see the Irish woman living in the house, and Mother Elisabeth thought that perhaps they meant Sister Katherine, who had an Irish surname, Flanagan. She sent for her, but after looking her up and down in her Bridgettine robes, they announced that this was not the woman they sought. Was there anyone else? Somebody suddenly through of a quiet, devout lady who was staying with them, a Miss Violet Gibson. Could she be the one? Yes, that was the name—and they demanded to see her room. She was out, and her trunk was locked, but they smashed it open and went through her things. The nuns watched in some horror as the police confiscated everything—clothes, some religious tracts, money and jewellery. Finally, they found her passport, and since this meant that she could not have left the country, they agreed to give some more information and to answer the nuns' repeated questions. Miss Gibson had that day attempted to shoot Mussolini.

> We could not believe it was possible. Miss Gibson was one of the quietest and sweetest of persons, refined, gentle, considerate of others

in every way! She lived the life of a poor
Franciscan, though she had means enough to
live very comfortably. (It was said that she went
around with a shopping-bag filled with paper-
bills, *lire*[1] which she gave out right and left,
going through the worst sections of the city,
poorly dressed — and it was in this bag that she
had concealed her revolver!)

Finally, the detectives left, leaving one man in
Miss Gibson's room. Later, the Commissioner
of Police arrived with 20 policemen, saying they
had come to 'protect' us. He told us that several
houses had been wrecked, and riots had taken
place, led by the fanatical followers of *Il Duce*...[2]

In those pre-television, pre-internet days, when a
household of nuns did not necessarily connect daily
with any news bulletins, no one at the St Birgitta
convent had heard of the uproar in the city that had
taken place that day. Miss Gibson had indeed shot
Mussolini — through the nose! He was not badly hurt,
though he bled profusely. Immediately a great assas-
sination plot was assumed. Miss Gibson was arrested
and her address at the Bridgettine house was discovered.

The Commissioner began to make an examina-
tion of all the Sisters and guests, beginning at
8.30pm and going on until past midnight. We
feared that the Fascists would make a raid on
our house during the night. We were questioned closely by the detectives, on various
other occasions and our Mother had to go to the
Palace of Justice to be questioned by the Judge.

In one sense, the sisters had not been incorrect in
seeing Miss Gibson as simply a quiet, well-behaved

lady. She had, by all accounts, spent most of her time in Rome quietly at the convent, doing jigsaws with her maid. She was the daughter of a former Lord Chancellor of Ireland, from a traditional Unionist and Protestant family and had spent her early adult life as part of the Anglo-Irish social scene, going to balls and dances and parties. But she was a lone spirit, wandering her own way—she became interested in different religions, dabbling in theosophy and eventually becoming a Catholic of a very intense kind. On one occasion she was seen wandering around Kensington with a kitchen knife in her hand, having left her Bible open at the story of Abraham sacrificing Isaac. By the time she left for Rome her closest friend Enid was pretty certain she intended to kill some one there. Enid thought the intended victim was probably the Pope.

On the day of her attack on Mussolini, she had risen at six, and been at Mass in the morning with the nuns, and then at breakfast. But Mother Riccarda had been a little concerned about her, because during the night she had complained of stomach pains, and Mother Riccarda had given her some medicine, and 'noticed that she had been reading an Italian newspaper, and had marked up some passages'. After breakfast, she announced that she was going out, and when asked she would be back for lunch she said she would, with a 'half smile'. Concerned, Mother Elisabeth watched from the convent window as Miss Gibson set off across the piazza. [3]

After her attempt on Mussolini, Miss Gibson was attacked by the mob and badly beaten. She was arrested and photographed, her faced 'swollen from punches and her expression oddly gentle and dignified.'[4] Unfortunately the threat to Mussolini's life made him more popular than before, not only in Italy but overseas, and this did not change until his invasion of Abyssinia almost a decade later, in 1935.

Meanwhile Miss Gibson was held in custody and her brother—himself an extremely eccentric character with a passionate commitment to Irish nationalism who was seen 'wandering around the Colosseum in a saffron-coloured kilt'[5] came to escort her home. It had become clear that she was mentally deranged, and instead of being imprisoned she was taken back to Britain where she spent the rest of her life in an asylum.

But over the next years the absurdity of this incident would give way to different events as Italy and the rest of Europe drew steadily nearer to war.

During the 1930s the sisters finally acquired the ownership of the original St Birgitta house in the Piazza Farnese, and after so many moves were able to settle there and make it their home. This fulfilled a long-cherished dream of Mother Elisabeth, but she could not have foreseen the extraordinary use to which the house would be put in the coming years of war.

By 1939 Mother Elisabeth was getting old—she was nearly 70—and she had never had good health. Much responsibility fell on the shoulders of her deputy, Mother Riccarda.

In the early years of the war the Bridgettine sisters assisted various people who were homeless or refugees. Italy was neutral for the first ten months of the war, but declared war on France and Britain only when it looked as though Germany would be swiftly victorious. Italian soldiers became engaged in fighting the British in Eritrea and Somalia. Conditions back in Italy became more difficult, with food shortages and general hardship.

In March 1941 Mother Katherine died in Sweden and was buried at Vastena. Because she was so much loved for her kindness and gentleness—even in her last letters she was begging forgiveness of anyone she had ever offended—she was very much mourned, and people were starting to speak of her as a saint.

In Rome, the sisters were increasingly caught up in the drama of war. In July and August 1943 the city was bombed. Several hundred people were killed. At St Birgitta's the sisters took to the basement when the air-raid sirens went. There was a small chapel there, which they had dedicated to St Richard Reynolds, the English martyr after whom Sister Riccarda had been named.

In due course it would not just be the sisters and a few visitors who were living at St Birgitta's. What had been a quiet comfortable guest-house became a place where people in desperate need came because they were at risk of their lives.

The people most in need were the Jews. When the Nazis occupied Italy after the fall of Mussolini in 1943, German troops arrived in all the major cities. This spelled a direct threat to Jewish families, as the policy of the Nazis in every occupied country was to hunt out Jews and arrest them, sending them in large numbers to by train to an unknown destination in Eastern Europe. The only escape was to go into hiding.

> On October 16, the Germans combed the houses and streets of Rome in search of Jews who, regardless of age, sex or health were taken to the Collegio Militare. A few days earlier, Pope Pius XII had personally ordered the Vatican clergy to open the sanctuaries of Vatican City to all 'non-Aryans' in need of refuge. By the

> morning of October 16, a total of 477 Jews had
> been given shelter in the Vatican and its
> enclaves, while another 4,238 had been given
> sanctuary in the many monasteries and con-
> vents in Rome.[6]

But in that first round-up, 1015 Jews who had not
reached shelter in time were caught. "Held for two
days in the Collegio Militare, they were then deported
to Auschwitz" and only 16 of them would survive the
war.[7]

The Piperno family, a Jewish family whose home
was in Siena, would find a refuge with the Bridgettines.

The first pressures on Jewish people had come with
anti-Jewish laws which imposed restrictions over a
whole range of everyday activities. Piero Piperno, then
a teenager, remembers the sequence of events very
clearly. 'It was a series of systematic restrictions. Jews
could not own radios. Jews could not be listed in the
telephone directory. If a Jewish person died, his obit-
uary could not be published. It was like Kafka's
Metamorphosis: you wake up one day and discover that
you have become an insect.'[8]

Piero and his three sisters and their widowed
mother, together with an aunt and some cousins, were
helped by two women who worked for the family.
They helped them to get to Rome, and arrangements
were made for them to go to the Bridgettine sisters.

> In Siena we lived in a road dedicated to St
> Catherine—because it led up to St Catherine's
> Church—and then in Rome we went to St
> Birgitta's. I have always found that intriguing,
> because I know the two saints are connected.

At first my mother did not tell Mother Elisabeth Hesselblad that we were Jews. There were a lot of refugees in Rome—people fleeing there to escape the bombing and the fighting elsewhere. My mother liked Mother Elisabeth very much. They got on well and enjoyed each other's company. They were both intelligent women. I think my mother, a courageous woman who was raising her children alone as a widow in wartime, really found a sort of soul-mate in Mother Elisabeth.

One day my mother said to me: 'Mother Elisabeth is some one to whom it is impossible to tell a lie. She is some one to whom one has to tell the truth.' And she told her that we were Jews. I remember this well, because at Christmas we had gone to all the Masses in the chapel, behaving very devoutly, kneeling there properly. But now Mother Elisabeth said to us—and I still find this very moving, I still find myself choking a bit as I talk about it—that we must live our own beliefs, that we should not feel any need to pretend, and that we must live and pray as Jews. That was very courageous, and very forward-looking: it was not at all the way that most Catholics thought at that time.[9]

He was just fifteen years old. No one quite knew, at that stage, exactly what the Nazis were doing to the Jews, but there were rumours of camps 'in the east' and of mass killings. In fact, a decision had already been taken by the Nazis in Berlin to kill all the Jews in Europe, and camps such as Auschwitz were established as extermination centres: eventually some six million would die.

The nuns, said Piperno, 'gave us back our dignity'. They treated them as guests who were welcomed. 'It's impossible to explain what that meant to us. We felt human again.'

Food was very scarce, and everyone went hungry. Piperno remembers:

We mostly had vegetable soup. It was rather thin and didn't have much in it sometimes. I remember saying to my mother that I thought Mother Riccarda went out into the Piazza Farnese and picked the grass and herbs there, because that's all there seemed to be in it. I do remember being hungry a lot of the time. Sometimes at night I would lie unable to sleep simply because I was hungry.

> There was no question of saying 'I don't like this — I don't want it'. If I took something from a dish and then put it on my plate, I had to eat all of it. But I didn't have a problem with that: I was hungry — I ate absolutely everything I could.

There were at that time a total of 13 Jewish adults and children in the house. The men slept in one room, except for one of Piero's uncles who had a small room to himself which others did not want as it was dark and had no windows. The women had two other rooms. They all came together for meals, which Mother Riccarda brought to them.

> My cousin was able to go out and about a bit, because he didn't look too Jewish. But the rest of us had to stay in the house all the time. But we weren't too restricted — we had the use of several rooms and could go from room to room. I did go out just one time, when I had to visit the dentist. This was a relation of ours, who was still working in Rome. It was safe to go to him,

because he knew who we were. Incidentally, he was also the dentist for Pius XII!

I was even able to continue my education: a lady professor, a Jewish lady, came in and gave me lessons. She taught me Latin. We studied Tactitus and I became really engrossed in it. It was particularly important for me, because earlier the Jews had been kicked out of all the schools, and I could have missed out on the chance of an education. But because of this tutoring, when the Allies arrived and we were liberated, I hadn't missed a year of my schooling.[10]

The rooms that the family were using were actually in the Sisters' private quarters, as this was the safest place. Unknown to the 15-year-old Piperno, they narrowly escaped being raided. On one occasion a German officer insisted on inspecting the house. Mother Elisabeth allowed him to look in the guest area but refused him admittance to the sisters' private section: 'We are nothing but a group of defenceless women, living in a convent. I do not believe that a German officer will violate our privacy.' It was a war of wills, and he went away.[11]

The convent and its church stand on one side of the Piazza Farnese, and across the square stood a police station. This meant that there was constant police activity with cars arriving and departing, often with considerable shouting and noise, causing no small alarm to those sheltering with the Bridgettines.

Piperno remembers Mother Elisabeth as being a quite formidable character, and very much the leader of the community. Mother Riccarda was a much more quiet and reserved character. 'What I remember most about Mother Riccarda was her smile. She was so sweet and kind always, and her smile was beautiful, radiant. She helped everyone—you instinctively went to her when you were troubled, and she would soothe things. She was also very pretty—you can't tell that from her photograph, but in real life she was really beautiful. She was English—very much so!—but she had fluent Italian. She put everyone at ease. We called her *Mamima*—Little Mother.'

> In a way you could say she was rather in the shadow of Mother Elisabeth, who was definitely the lady in charge and who had a big personality. Our Mamima, Mother Riccarda, was different— she quiet, she did things in a quiet pleasant way. We all loved her very much.[12]

Reverend Mother Thekla who today (2013) is superior of the community at St Birgitta's, and who joined the community in 1950, echoes this. She knew Mother Riccarda well: 'She was truly very beautiful. She was a wonderful person—an angel on the earth. And she was humble—she had this spirit of service, of simply wanting to serve and help people.'

> Above all she had a profound respect for these Jewish guests. It was very important not to let them feel in any way humiliated by their situation—they were vulnerable, and it was crucial to let them know that they were welcome and that the sisters wanted to help them in any way they could. They were a wonderful family and they became very good friends of the Sisters. Some still come back every year for a reunion.
>
> Mother Riccarda was an extremely discreet woman—she knew when to talk and when not to talk, she was gentle and calm. And she was highly educated: she spoke good German, so

she was able to speak with confidence to German soldiers if they came around. She was in fact fluent in three or four languages—which didn't seem remarkable at the time because it was an essential part of the international character of the community.

The police and other authorities respected the Bridgettines. 'Here in the Piazza Farnese we had this big house—everyone knew us. I think that helped to give the Bridgettines some protection. And then Mother Riccarda was English—people respected that.'[13]

Unknown to most of the other occupants of the house, a young soldier who had deserted from the German army was also hiding there.

Vello Salo was a young Estonian who had been drafted into the German Army and sent to fight in Italy. He absconded and was hidden by the nuns. Later he became a priest. Now aged 87, he looks back down the years:

> In the faraway year 1945, I spent three weeks in the Casa di Santa Brigida and I'm sure I owe my vocation to priesthood to the prayer of the good sisters, including Mother Riccarda. Now, all sisters knew about the one refugee living in St. Richard's chapel and were warned not to talk about him, but the refugee did not meet all sisters: blessed Mother Elisabeth took good care of my wellbeing, Sister Giuseppina taught me Italian... these two are the only names I remember.[14]

Discretion, silence, and courage ensured everyone's safety. Piero Piperno recalls 'There was great solidarity, because everybody was suffering and everybody finally realised we were all in the same boat.'[15]

The connection with Sweden, as a neutral country, also gave all at St Birgitta's an extra measure of safety. At the front door, the sisters placed a notice announcing that the house was Swedish territory. This was never tested legally, but it certainly sent out a confident message to the German forces, and although there were some visits from the German Army, the house was never searched and they were for the most part left alone.

The Piperno family stayed with the sisters for six months. Piero Piperno recalls 'I remember it all exactly, because the day we went from Sienna to Rome was my uncle's birthday—15 November—and then the day the Allies came was 4 June, which was my cousin's birthday. That was the day we were liberated.'

They had all been listening to the BBC, broadcasting from London, every day, and so knew that the Allies were getting nearer and nearer to them. But the situation was confused and uncertain, and no one really knew what was happening in Rome.

> Then a truck arrived. They were French sol-
> diers. They got out and knocked on the front
> door. They called out 'We are French, of de
> Gaulle!' So we knew they were the Free French,
> they were the Allies. And all the lights of the
> house went on, and stayed on for ten minutes.
> And lights came on all across Rome at the same
> time. We were free! But everything was still
> confused. The front line of battle was still
> moving: everything was dangerous. In fact a
> relation of mine was killed elsewhere in Rome
> on that very day—the very last member of our
> family to die in the war.[16]

Notes

1. This was the Italian currency before the Euro.
2. Sister Reginalda's diary, quoted in M. Tjader, *The Most Extraordinary Woman in Rome* (Generalate House, Sisters of St Bridget, 1987), p. 164.
3. F. S. Saunders, *The Woman who shot Mussolini* (London: Faber and Faber 2010), p. 4.
4. Review of *The Woman who shot Mussolini*. Freya Johnston, Telegraph Media Group 26 Feb , 2010, www.telegraph.co.uk
5. Review of *The Woman who Shot Mussolini*, The Times, 29 August 2009.
6. M. Gilbert *The Holocaust* (London: Fontana/Collins, 1986), p. 623.
7. *Ibid.*
8. Interview with the author, Rome July 2012.
9. *Ibid.*
10. *Ibid.*
11. M. Tjader *The Most Extraordinary Woman in Rome* (Rome: Generalate House, Sisters of St Bridget, 1987), p. 198.
12. Interview with the author, Rome, 2012.
13. Interview with the author, Rome, 2010.
14. Correspondence with author, June 2012.
15. *The Times* (29 August 2009).
16. Interview with the author, Rome, 2012.

CHAPTER EIGHT

HEN THE ALLIES arrived in Rome, there was great rejoicing. But the situation was confused and remained so for some while.

'There were houses left empty by Fascist families who fled' Piero Piperno recalls

> And some of us were re-housed there. Meanwhile the Sisters were still helping people. I learned later that in those days at the end of the war they sheltered the families of Fascists. At first that bothered me. But I now believe that they were right to do that because these were just families: there were children in need.

The sisters joined in the general post-war relief efforts and the distribution of food and clothing sent to them via Swedish agencies. Long queues of people formed outside the convent, and the sisters worked daily to distribute supplies. Clothes that were sent were taken up to the flat roof terrace for washing, mending and sorting. They even featured in a Swedish film with actress Ingrid Bergman, where their story was told to help raise funds for *Save the Children*, and Swedish newspapers also published pictures showing Mother Elisabeth and Mother Riccarda.

The nuns' heroism in helping to save the lives of Jewish children was part of the inspiration for the film *Conspiracy of Hearts* starring Lilli Palmer, Sylvia Syms, Yvonne Mitchell and David Kossoff.

The Piperno family kept in touch with Mother Elisabeth and the community. Piero Piperno went on to complete his education and then worked at various jobs over the next years, becoming a farmer and an estate agent and, for a while, a hospital administrator. He married, and had two sons and now has four grandchildren. In 1956 his mother died and in 1976 his brother. He is now the representative of the family keeping in touch with the Sisters.

> After the war, whatever work was available, you took it. We didn't expect things to be easy—we were prepared to work hard.

> Now, long years later, I am essentially a full-time grandfather. At school my grandchildren were taught about the Holocaust and every year they honour January 27th, the day the Russians liberated Auschwitz, as a Day of Memory. The teacher asked me if I would go in and speak to the children, and I did so. We had cousins who died in the Holocaust, and school friends.

> When I look back to the time in the Bridgettine house I remember the friendship, the courtesy, the solidarity. What I want to tell the children about is how people helped each other: I want them to learn about that and not only about how we were persecuted. I try to teach them: act towards others as you would want them to act towards you.

In the post-war years, with Mother Elisabeth in increasing poor health, more responsibility fell on Mother Riccarda, who was also now approaching her seventies. The Bridgettine Order continued to grow— the houses in England and in Sweden and Switzerland flourished, and there was also a growing one in India.

In 1957 Mother Elisabeth died, having the previous year celebrated her Golden Jubilee—fifty years as a nun in the service of the Church. She was buried at the Verano cemetery in Rome, but a year later permission was given to bury her in St Birgitta's church, next door to the convent where she had lived and worked. She was beatified in 2000 by Pope John Paul II and in 2004 was honoured in Israel by being named 'Righteous among the gentiles' at Yad Vashem, the Holocaust memorial at Jerusalem. She is one of ten Swedish people thus honoured.

The Righteous whose names are inscribed at Yad Vashem are described by Holocaust survivor Primo Levi in the literature and on the website:

> The price that rescuers had to pay for their action differed from one country to another. In Eastern Europe, the Germans executed not only the people who sheltered Jews, but their entire family as well. Notices warning the population against helping the Jews were posted everywhere. Generally speaking punishment was less severe in Western Europe, although there too the consequences could be formidable and some of the Righteous Among the Nations were incarcerated in camps and killed. Moreover, seeing the brutal treatment of the Jews and the determination on the part of the perpetrators to hunt down every single Jew, people must have feared that they would suffer greatly if they attempted to help the persecuted. In consequence, rescuers and rescued lived under constant fear of being caught; there was always the danger of denunciation by neighbours or collaborators.[1]

Mother Riccarda took Mother Elisabeth's place as Abbess General of the order in 1958. Everything was still expanding, and a new foundation was created in America. Bridgettines were increasingly interested in ecumenical work with Christians of other denominations, a new house was opened in Assisi, and the flow of visitors to the house in Rome did not cease.

Mother Riccarda died in 1966, much loved and honoured. She had by this time very few close relatives. Her brother Basil had served — at Dunkirk and elsewhere — in World War II having managed to rejoin the Army although he was over age. After the war, he lived for many years in Kenya, where he owned Wispers Farm, near Nairobi. By his fourth marriage, he had a daughter, Everild Tania Hambrough, who was born and brought up in Kenya, and she married Major William Coleridge, 5th Baron Coleridge, in 1962.

Lord Coleridge recalls 'Basil, my father-in-law, was a wonderful character. There was great hospitality at Wispers Farm, and he had had a remarkable life, serving in both world wars…we knew he had a sister who was a nun, and I think he did get to Rome to visit her once. But it was expensive and complicated to make that sort of trip in those early years after the war. I think he was quite proud of her — but they were leading very different lives and during the war he would of course not have been able to make any contact with each other at all.'[2]

The Coleridge's first child, Tania, was born in January 1966 and so for the last few months of her life, Mother Riccarda had a small great-niece, although she never saw her.[3] There are now other great-nephews and nieces, and they have families too.

But for most of Mother Riccarda's adult life her real family had been the Bridgettine sisters. They were to cherish her memory, and especially her wartime courage in the service of refugees, for whom she risked her life. Some forty years after her death the announcement came from Rome of her possible beatification, and that of Mother Katherine Flanagan.

The parishes in Britain with which these women are associated—St Mary Magdalen's in Brighton where Mother Riccarda was baptised, and St Gregory's at Earlsfield where Mother Katherine grew up—are excited about the honour.

Fr John Henry of St Gregory's said that Mother Katherine was a woman with great dedication and 'willingness to up and go to strange countries at a moment's notice and commence new initiatives and make new foundations'. He has collected together information about her life and that of Fr Benedict Williamson, whose deep interest in the Bridgettines was actually responsible for these two women going to Rome to help re-found the Order.

Many of those who worked closely with Mother Katherine left testimonies to her kindness, love, and generosity. She has also left some writings and prayers. She was particularly noted for her willing obedience— as a woman of considerable skill and organising ability, she never asserted her own importance or showed the slightest desire to affirm her own status over others, but always saw herself as a member of a community who had made a solemn vow to obey her superiors. When she learned that she was seriously ill she wrote to Mother Elisabeth in Rome explaining the situation and saying 'What does my beloved mother wish me to do? Give orders and your child is ready'.

She was also calm about the abandonment of plans for her to go to America, a project which they had hoped to develop when the Second World War was

over. She wrote 'God's holy will be done. If he wants
me to die before I go to America he will send some one
else. God is so good, he gives me time to prepare for
death.'

Mother Riccarda is still remembered by those who
worked with her. Elisa Famiglietti, spokesman for the
Bridgettines in Rome, said: 'Mother Riccarda was a
wonderful woman. I knew her well and met her in
1954 and was with her up until her death in 1966.

> She was an angel who did so much to help our
> Jewish brothers during the war and I know they
> want to honour her as well. There are about a
> dozen or so sisters here in the convent in Rome
> who remember her and we are all very excited
> at the fact she is being considered for sainthood.
>
> Mother Riccarda was full of the spirit of God
> and was a very humble woman, she sang
> beautifully from the heart and she was devoted
> to God and she left a mark on all of us.
>
> Mother Riccarda was humble and discreet and
> she provided safety and charity for our Jewish
> brothers during the war but she very rarely
> spoke about it.
>
> What I always remember about her is that
> despite living for so long in Italy she never
> forgot she was English and always spoke
> English to us.[4]

With the possible beatification of Mothers Katherine
and Riccarda, the house of St Birgitta in Rome will, be
in the extraordinary position of having being home to
no less than three women at the same time who are to
be honoured by the Church as being of unusual
sanctity.

Part of the tradition of the Catholic Church is that saints inspire localised devotion. St Gregory's church in Earlsfield where Katherine Flanagan worshipped was destroyed in World War II and later rebuilt. It is packed for Mass every Sunday, and afterwards families meet to chat in the big church hall. This is a different London from the one that she knew—since the 1960s large numbers of immigrants from the West Indies and from Asia have settled here and a typical Sunday gathering sees a big mix of races. The parish is proud of its links with a possible new saint, and Father John Henry has been gathering information about Kitty Flanagan to build up a picture of her to share with future generations of parishioners.

At St Mary Magdalen's in Brighton parish priest Fr Ray Blake is already talking of the creation of a shrine, commenting that 'Brighton needs tons of saints but more importantly this is excellent for Catholic-Jewish relations. Her canonisation would demonstrate what many Catholics who didn't hit the news were actually doing in the Second World War. They were trying to live Christian lives in very fraught times often at great risk to themselves."[5]

There is considerable local interest in Mother Riccarda, and a local bus has been named in her honour! It was blessed by Fr Blake, in a ceremony outside St Mary Magdalen's church where Mother Riccarda was baptised over a hundred years earlier. The bus, run by the Brighton and Hove corporation, is a double-decker, Number 7, the route that goes to the Brighton Marina on the sea-front.

At Ventnor on the Isle of Wight, there are still traces of the Hambrough family's legacy: there is a Hambrough Road and a Hambrough House hotel. Staff at the hotel were intrigued to know of the link with this courageous Bridgettine nun, as was the vicar of St Catherine's church, founded by the Hambrough family.[6]

The Bridgettine convent in Rome is a popular guest house which welcomes many visitors every year. There are memorials to Mother Elisabeth, Mother Riccarda and Mother Katherine Flanagan in the sunny courtyard where guests are often entertained. The Sisters play a very active part in the life of the Church in Rome. In 1991 they took part in a special celebration for the 600th anniversary of the canonisation of St Birgitta, in which the Lutheran Primates of Sweden and Finland joined with Pope John Paul II for Vespers. The Bridgettine sisters accompanied the Pope and the Primates, carrying candles, in procession to the High Altar, and the sisters placed candles along the semicircular rail surrounding the tomb of St Peter while a packed congregation sang 'O Joyful Light'. It was the first time that Catholic and Lutheran leaders had prayed together in St Peter's. Queen Silvia of Sweden proclaimed one of the Scripture readings.[7]

In 2010 Pope Benedict XVI formally declared Mother Riccarda and Mother Katherine 'Venerable' in a ceremony in Rome. This is the first stage on the way to possible Beatification.

There are Bridgettine sisters today on four continents.

> In keeping with the monastic tradition, the Bridgettine sisters' chief obligation is liturgical prayer, the regular Divine Office. The sisters take part daily in Holy Mass and there is Adoration of the Blessed Sacrament every day. Central to the sisters' work is the Guest House

which is part of the activity of Bridgettine sisters
... The sisters' hospitality is an answer to the
needs of many pilgrims.[8]

The sisters seek to respond to the needs of the Church:
they have a special concern for ecumenical contacts,
bringing together Christians of different traditions,
and in some countries also work as catechists, run
nursery schools, and provide housing for students and
old people.

The Bridgettine sisters in Britain include a community in Birmingham, where they run the accommodation for students at the Maryvale Institute, a Catholic
distance-learning college, and a house at Holywell in
Wales for pilgrims.

The stories of Katherine Flanagan and Riccarda
Hambrough are part of the wider story of Catholic
women down the centuries.

> The moral and spiritual strength of a woman is
> joined to her awareness that God entrusts the
> human being to her in a special way. Of course,
> God entrusts every human being to each and
> every other human being. But this entrusting
> concerns women in a special way — precisely by
> reason of their femininity — and this in a partic-
> ular way determines their vocation.

> The moral force of women, which draws
> strength from this awareness, and this entrust-
> ing, expresses itself in a great number of figures
> of the Old Testament, of the time of Christ, and
> of later ages right up to our own day.[9]

Notes

1   Yad Vashem website: www.1yadvashem.org

2   Conversation with the author, 2012.

3   This great-niece is Tania Harcourt-Couze. She has three children, Evie, Sophia, and William.

4   *Catholic Herald* (13 February 2009).

5   *Daily Telegraph* (22 May 2010).

6   Conversations with the author, 2009 and 2010.

7   For a description of this service, see G. Weigel, *Witness to Hope* (London: HarperCollins, 1999), p. 592.

8   Bridgettine sisters' brochure (United Kingdom, 2012).

9   Blessed John Paul II, *Mulieris Dignitatem*, Apostolic Letter on the dignity and vocation of women (1988), 30.

Lightning Source UK Ltd.
Milton Keynes UK
UKOW03f0341030614

232743UK00001B/4/P